Dating Disasters

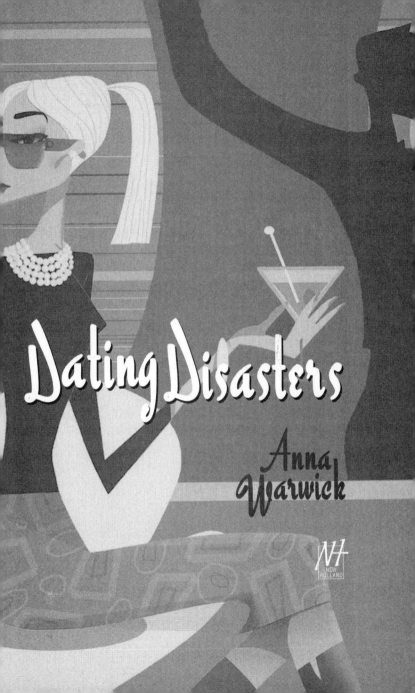

Dating Disasters

Anna Warwick

NH
NEW
HOLLAND

First published in Australia in 2004 by
New Holland Publishers (Australia) Pty Ltd
Sydney • Auckland • London • Cape Town

14 Aquatic Drive Frenchs Forest NSW 2086 Australia
218 Lake Road Northcote Auckland New Zealand
86 Edgware Road London W2 2EA United Kingdom
80 McKenzie Street Cape Town 8001 South Africa

National Library of Australia Cataloguing-in-Publication Data:
Warwick, Anna (Annabelle Jean), 1975—.
Dating disasters.
ISBN 1 74110 139 5.
1. Dating (Social customs). I. Title.

306.73

Publishing Manager: Robynne Millward
Project Editor: Liz Hardy
Designer: Nanette Backhouse
Production Manager: Kellie Matterson
Printed in Australia by McPherson's Printing Group, Victoria
Cover image courtesy of Getty Images
10 9 8 7 6 5 4 3 2 1

Contents

Introduction

In a world full of lonely people it would be terribly selfish to be lonely alone.

Tennessee Williams

I love dating. I love meeting new boys and making new friends. Don't get me wrong; I am not the most social person on earth and I don't click with everybody—but that's the funny part.

We are all individuals these days, which is why single life makes sense, and why we are all so fascinating and strange to each other.

I don't understand the war of the sexes. I mean boy + girl = how hard can it be? We all work, play and sleep; we all need cuddles; and it's hard and scary for everyone. Any differences at all between us should be celebrated (life would be so boring without them). But it has been an *issue* for centuries, and probably always will be.

If a relationship is the way two people relate, then every individual you meet will offer you a different relationship. Since there are billions of us humans, the possibilities are endless! And let's face it, we're not chasing woolly mammoths any more so why not chase each other? It's not a life or death adventure but it sure can feel like it!

Dating is not just about looking for *The One*; it's all about getting out of your comfort zone and making an unlikely connection.

Some people love being single. It's especially fun to be single when you have friends of the opposite sex to hang out with. To be honest I wouldn't have many friends of the opposite sex if I hadn't tried dating them first. Now I can't do without them.

Even if you are looking for *The One*, it is very hard to squeeze a relationship in when you're working full-time, having an active social life, keeping fit, pursuing new hobbies and keeping up with the rellos. The occasional date can give you a shot of romance and really boost your mojo. Things don't always have to end in tears—honesty from the start ('I'm not looking for a relationship and I don't have time for one') is the key.

Of course dating can be scary! You might start talking about pets and it turns out they just accidentally ran over their pedigree cat and squished it all over their driveway. Or you might spray chardonnay out of your nose when laughing…Anything can go wrong at any time and then you're stuck there smiling politely through dessert…

It's worth it for the gory horror stories, you can dine out on them for months.

If a relationship is fun, like a friendship, it will be worth working on and keeping, but it takes time to find that kind of connection. On the way you might get a few pashes, yummy meals, shags, laughs and probably a few hangovers. And yeah, there may be a few Saturday nights when you come home from another disastrous date and just want to cry because you're thinking you're a *freak magnet* and it's been going on for too long and you will probably be *alone for eternity*…or at least until your best friend wakes up in four hours and you can cry down the phone to them.

And if you are stuck at home on Saturday night *do* something about it or just admit that you're happy in front of the TV in your trackie dacks and with a large pizza all to yourself. There are dating web sites, nightclubs, pubs, trivia nights, bingo evenings, RSL clubs, festivals, dance classes, concerts, cafes, cinemas etc. Don't just sit there moping, take action! Get out there and get amongst it. Next!

Akubra Girl

Ryan, 39

It was 1988. The National Dance Institute in New York was putting on this huge seaside spectacular at Madison Square Garden. The stage was the beach, and the audience was the ocean. All the little kids were dressed up as sea creatures. They had a shark and everything. The director said, 'I know, get me some of those bronzed Aussie surfers from Down Under'. So they called up the Bondi Surf Life Saving Club and invited our entire surf team over.

I was 24 and I was in New York with all my best mates. We were actually *dancing* on Broadway. They gave us 1500 bucks US for spending money, and sent us to Tahiti for a week beforehand to get a tan! And the gorgeous girls from the National Dancing Institute who were assigned to look after us…of course we all fell in love, you know.

They took us to Yankee Stadium and they took us out to Coney Island and it was just great, you know? Young surfers, we were decked out in all this fancy gear; we had the camel blazers and the Driza-bones and the hats—big Akubra hats—and everything.

This was in the days of Crocodile Dundee, Australia was huge, and Akubra hats…well…little did we know it, but all these ballet chicks were sizing up the gear!

The girl I was with was called Mary. Mary and I went out one night to Yankee Stadium to watch the Yankees play. Then we went back to her Lower East Side apartment. I thought, 'Oooh this is all *very* good'. But afterwards I had to get back to the hotel because we had a big show to do the next day, so I put my clothes back on, said, 'See you tomorrow', and left.

Now the thing you didn't want to lose was your Akubra hat, 'cause your Akubra hat was deadset your ticket to anywhere. And the next morning I couldn't find it…and Mary wouldn't answer my calls or let me back into her apartment. I didn't have a hat to wear in the show, people stopped coming up to me on the street—it was like Superman losing his power.

I looked Mary up last time I was over there and a friend of hers told me that she's now an archaeologist, like Indiana Jones. She married some professor. I bet she wears that bloody hat every time she goes out on a dig.

Tonight? I'm sorry, but… I have to floss my cat.

13

Ice Man

Bridget, 30

This was up in Brisbane a long time ago. Richard came and picked me up, he was a stockbroker. As we were driving to the restaurant I asked a question and he answered, 'Negative, Ghost Rider'. And I sort of didn't say anything because I was thinking, 'Did he just say, "Negative, Ghost Rider?" That's kind of weird, isn't it?'

Then when we were parking the car under his work, he saw a colleague who was just leaving. The colleague asked him if we were going to the work party, and Richard leaned out the window and for a second time said, 'Negative, Ghost Rider'. And I remember thinking that we hadn't even got to the restaurant and I'd already had two Negative, Ghost Riders. I thought it was a bit wankerish but figured I'd give it a go, because I always just dumped boys at the drop of a hat.

So we went into the most beautiful restaurant and we had the best food, the best wine, this guy was hot. Everything was going so well until…Richard said, 'Now I want to ask you a question. It's a question I ask everybody I meet and it's how I judge your character.' And I waited for some really important question on religion or something…and he just got all serious and stared into my eyes and said, 'Did you cry when Goose died in *Top Gun*?'

Can you believe a boy did this to me?

And I went, 'Yeah, what's your question?' And he goes, 'That's the question'. And I just died, I had to go into the toilet and call my girlfriend with a 'date update', I told her I was at dinner with Ice Man. It was terrible; she was wetting her pants laughing.

And still to this day if we're at the pub and I ask her if she wants a beer she will turn around and say 'Negative, Ghost Rider'...and we still wet our pants over it. How could a boy be so weird?

Tonight? I'm sorry, but...I'm trying to see how long I can go without saying yes.

An Innocent Date

Nicholas, 25

There was this chick I'd been interested in for years, she was my best friend's sister. I always thought she was too young for me, but finally one day she decided to ask me out. I was amazed. She had a body that any man would want, killer eyes and a soft voice—that just turned me on.

She still lived at home with her parents, trying to save some money before moving out. I respected that, of course. We ended up going out to a movie and dinner—very simple and innocent. But she was making me nervous with the way she would curl up to me during the movie.

When we went to dinner, I told her how long I had been admiring her. She said she felt the same way. In the middle of our dinner, I excused myself to go to the bathroom. All I could think about was how nervous I was, but at the same time so comfortable with her. I wasn't paying attention to anything but her.

I returned to the table and we chatted for hours. Finally, we headed back to her house. We drove up her driveway and talked some more. I wondered whether I should make a move.

So, I kissed her softly and she started to kiss me harder and more passionately. She moved over to my side of the car and put her arms around me. Then, in the heat of the moment—just my luck—she kicked her drink onto the passenger side floor and grabbed some napkins to clean it up.

As soon as she ducked below the dashboard to clean up the mess, the house lights came on and her parents rushed out of the house to the car. Her father came to my car window and her mother went to her daughter's window. They stood there staring at us. The father asked me to come inside, and said that he would like to talk to me. I told him that would be great!

We all sat down in the living room. I told them all about our evening, but her father had a disgusted look on his face as I talked. In the middle of the conversation, he stormed out of the room. I was getting scared at this point!

He called his daughter in a loud and very parental voice. The mother sat me down and started to tell me that her husband was very protective of his daughter and they would not stand for her to be used. I agreed with her. Then she threw a family album in my lap and started to show me baby pictures of their daughter. As I was looking at these pictures, I noticed something…I had forgotten to zip up my pants when I went to the bathroom at the restaurant! Then, everything made sense to me. I started to look at it from the parents' point of view…they saw us kissing in the car, then their daughter bent over in her seat to clean up the spilled drink, and now this—an unzipped fly! I'd never been so embarrassed in my life.

I got up and told the mother that I had enjoyed the talk but I had to run. I left straight away, never to ask her out again.

Tonight? I'm sorry, but…the Dalai Lama said he might drop in.

Aries Men

Naomi, 44

I met this guy at a huge party at a film studio—I was really straight at the party and everyone else was off their face. We made eye contact and then he came up to me and he was American (I like Americans, I have a thing about them) and he was cute—tall with dark hair.

He was being really nice and friendly—later I found out he'd been on half an ecstasy. He was telling me I was an angel and that he hadn't been attracted to anybody in ages, but we didn't kiss or anything.

It turned out he was in advertising, quite a big company. And I thought, 'Oh yeah, this is like way, way too good to be true'. But he took me out to a schwanky restaurant at the beach three nights later.

Dinner was fine. He was quite a good date—he was very attentive and he had excellent table manners.

Then he started talking about this girl that he'd broken up with recently. She was 24 or something, and couldn't handle the fact that he had children. And he couldn't handle the fact that she couldn't handle the children (he had two boys).

I started thinking, 'Okay maybe this guy isn't so perfect'. I mean, I can deal with two boys, but the 24-year-old model ex, I could not handle. And then he told me I was the first 'older woman' that he had been attracted to in a long, long time. So the pressure was on.

Anyway, I got a bit intense and I said, 'Oh why don't you come back to my place, it's just up the road'. I was nervous and sort of rushed things. We got to this point where we were kissing in my room and it was really nice but I could just tell that he wasn't really there. So I said, 'Your heart's not really in this, is it?' And he said, 'Ooh I don't know', and started talking about his ex-girlfriend again. I said, 'Well listen, you know you haven't been broken up with this girl for very long, I'll bet you're making comparisons. She's probably entering your mind—don't worry about it, it's completely what you'd expect.'

I felt so stupid, I should have known that he wouldn't be ready. I'm old enough to know that.

But it also completely reinforced the fact that when I had done his astrology I'd found out that he had *four* signs in Aries. In a man? That many planets in Aries? Hilarious! That combination makes people just insanely hot one minute, cold the next. It was amazing I'd even got to first base. And of course I never heard from him again.

He was just on ecstasy when we met and he actually believed himself at the time—typical Aries man!

Tonight? I'm sorry, but...I've been scheduled for a karma transplant.

The Answering Machine

Brian, 21

his incident got ugly before we even went out. One day at uni I met this really good-looking girl through some friends and we started talking. Eventually we agreed that we should go for a drink one day so we could get to know each other better.

A few days passed and I gave her a call to ask her out. She wasn't there so I left a message and went to happy hour with my flatmates. After a few hours and a few rounds of beers we returned home, only to discover that she had rung and left a message while we were gone.

So I called her back, but the phone rang and rang and eventually went to her answering machine. I left her another message and I hung up. Just then my slightly perverted and drunk flatmates started interrogating me about the girl and what she looked like.

So with a few beers swirling around in my body I mustered up the best description I could by saying, 'Oh…I don't know, but she has a really cute bum! I mean she has got this perfect arse, blah, blah, blah…' and then my flatmates started joining in with a few miscellaneous X-rated comments. And then I heard a sound…

Well it turned out that I didn't hang the fucking phone up properly and our whole conversation was recorded onto her answering machine! That terrible beeping sound a phone makes after you leave it off the hook for a while still sends shivers down my spine every time I hear it.

Well, of course she got the message and even after all my apologising she still didn't want to go out with me.

[Original story courtesy of geekcheek.com and dating.about.com.]

Tonight? I'm sorry, but...my subconscious says no.

Banana Boy

Kirstie, 36

I met Banana Boy at a cocktail bar at 1 am. I was wearing a very sexy tweed hat and looking like 'I'm all that'. I went to get a drink and this very cute, tall, dark, well-dressed boy came up to me and said, 'Oh you are so beautiful in that hat, you look gorgeous', I went, 'Mmhmm. Thank you', and he started to chat me up.

I ignored him at first. Then he said, 'I'm going to take you out for dinner'. My ears pricked up. I said, 'Dinner? Okay, yes.' I can always go out for dinner. And he said, 'Yes, but first I have to kiss you'. I said, 'Okay, kiss me then'. And he gave me a nice big kiss on the lips. It was a lovely kiss. Then he took a breath, and said, 'Hang on—I'll just check if that was real'. So he gave me another kiss, and said, 'Yep, gimme your number'.

The next day we went out for a drink at an up-market pub that was popular with divorcees—he lived nearby. He couldn't talk because he had lost his voice, so he was communicating with me by writing on coasters and whispering in my ear. I thought he was very strange and full-on, but he was really into me and he was giving me all these lovely compliments and I figured he was young and sexy, so I'd stick around and find out where it was going.

We ended up going for dinner a few days later. Except that it wasn't really dinner; it was more like more drinks. I think he had been out all night and all day, I don't know…he was a space cadet. So we had some oysters and champagne, then I took him back to my house and we fooled around and blah, blah, blah. Before he left he told me that he'd see me on Thursday and this time he really would take me out to dinner.

The next day I got a text message saying, 'I'm in love with you, you are so beautiful. I'm going to go home and *leepy* about Kirstie.' Leepy? What did that mean—sleeping? Dreaming? So he kept texting me and emailing back and forth, and he was like *full-on*.

Anyway Thursday night rolled around and I had to work back late, but I rushed home and got ready. He came over at eight, rolling drunk with his tie around the back of his head—he'd been at a work function. We were supposed to go out for dinner, so I asked him, 'Are you hungry? Lets go!' He went, 'Yeah!' and with that he ripped a banana from the fruit bowl and started scoffing it down.

By this stage the charm was really wearing off. When he had finished the banana I took him up the street to a trendy restaurant and bar in the middle of St Kilda. As soon as we got there Banana Boy started chatting up one of the waitresses. I said, 'Nice work sunshine, you right there? Taking another girl's number? We're supposed to be out on a date!' He made up some crap like, 'Oh yeah, I'm trying to catch up with this guy that she knows who owes me money'. 'Yeah right…' I said, 'that's fine'.

I knew the management there and they saw me and waved us over to their table. But then they actually said to me, 'Look this guy is so pissed he can hardly talk, please take him away from us'. I was so embarrassed and had to slink away with him.

I started thinking, 'I'm going to do a runner, this is just so embarrassing and this guy is full of it, he's just a dickhead. I'm going to get outta here.' So I went into the bathroom and then when the coast was clear I bolted.

The next day he sent me a bizarre apologetic email in German. So I sent him an email in reply; it was a beauty. I spent a good fifteen minutes writing it out and I just let him have it.

Needless to say I never heard from Banana Boy again.

Tonight? I'm sorry, but...I'm staying home to work on my cottage cheese sculpture.

Blinding Date

Leoni, 42

My friend said she had a really nice guy to set me up with so I decided to give it a try. The guy called me, and we agreed to meet at a bar about halfway between our houses. When he got there I was impressed that he was funny, friendly *and* nice-looking. We seemed to be 'clicking' and I was really excited to be having such a good date.

It started to get late. I said I needed to go home, and like a gentleman, he walked me to my car. We stood outside the car talking and, because he was going to get a cab home, I offered to give him a ride.

We drove and talked, and it was nice, just very friendly. I noticed he was fidgeting around quite a bit but I was looking out my window, concentrating on the road. When I eventually stopped at a set of lights and turned to him, I realised the guy had taken off his shirt! 'It's hot in here', he said.

I laughed nervously and asked him where he lived.

When we eventually arrived at his place I stopped the car and turned to look at him again. Lo and behold, he was now totally naked! He was sitting there with a big smile on his face, and a pretty obvious erection. I didn't know where to put my eyes, I was so shocked!

'So, do you want to come inside?' he asked. I told him that I

25

couldn't imagine anything worse and shouted at him to get dressed and get out of my car.

When I finally regained my composure, I gave him a lecture about proper dating etiquette. I told him a guy shouldn't take his clothes off before he's even kissed his date. So then, he tried to kiss me! I told him to get his clothes on or I was going to call the police. He got angry, put on his clothes and got out of the car.

My friend was mortified when I told her what he had done. She hasn't tried to set me up again and, needless to say, I haven't been on a blind date since.

Tonight? I'm sorry, but...I'm building a pig from a kit.

The Drug Hog

Narelle, 35

A couple of years ago I was living in the city and I was sort of in dating mode. I was seeing lots of different guys. This guy actually had the potential to be more than a date. He seemed like a really interesting guy, he was quite good-looking and he was a doctor, which I always think highly recommends a man.

I was at a party when he asked if I wanted to go out sometime.

So he picked me up at my place one night the next week, and as we walked towards the restaurant he spent about ten minutes telling me about the time that he smoked some strange cactus in Mexico and what a *fantastic* high it gave him. And I thought, well that's fair enough—people take drugs, and I have nothing against people taking drugs...

But it went on and on and all he did all night was talk about all the drugs he's taken. There was the peyote cactus in Mexico and there was the worm in the tequila bottle he'd eaten...far from the sophisticated evening I had been expecting, I was basically out with a Drug Hog.

The evening ended up with us going back to his car after dinner and driving off to some nightclub. While we were parked outside the club he pulled a soda siphon out from under the driver's seat and he said to me, 'Would you like to suck on this? It gives you an amazing high!'

And I just thought, 'You are such a dag!' So I said, 'No thank you very much'. And he—this nice, good-looking, doctor chap—started sucking on this soda siphon, getting off his face in a side street outside a nightclub in Kings Cross. At which point I said, 'Right, date's over!'

I said goodnight and went home from there, and brushed him off the next time he called.

Tonight? I'm sorry, but...I'm touring China with a wok band.

Bourbon Street

Tim, 36

So, I'm on holidays in New Orleans and I meet this nurse called Kelly in a bar on Bourbon Street, and she's absolutely stunning. We spend three or four hours together drinking and dancing. We're kissing and hugging and I ask her if I can come back to her house and she says no, because she has a flatmate. So I ask her if she wants to come back to my hotel room, and she says, 'No I'd better not. I'll drop you home.'

I'm staying literally one block from the bar and she's going off in the opposite direction, so I say, 'Well I'll just walk home'. But she gives me her number and we make a date for lunch the next day and I tell her I'll call her in the morning.

So I'm walking home on my own, and just twenty metres out of the pub someone comes up behind me and grabs my arm, and I don't know who it is, so I react by pulling away. And it's a cop, and he goes, 'What are you doing big guy?'

I'm completely pissed but I try to explain to the guy, 'Look I'm a foreign citizen. I don't know anyone…I'm just going back to my hotel.' He goes, 'No, you're too drunk, come with me'. So he throws me in the back of a police car and drives me to a police station. They frisk me, give me a medical and then they throw me in a cell with thirty-five other blokes, who are all absolutely stinking drunk.

29

After a few hours I start to sober up, and then a few more hours go by and morning comes. Eventually it's getting towards lunchtime and I'm supposed to call Kelly but I'm still stuck in the cell.

At around two in the afternoon they finally charge me with public drunkenness on Bourbon Street. They tell me that if I can't pay the bond—which is US$300—I'll have to stay in jail for another twenty-six hours. I don't have $300 on me.

They finally let me make a phone call so I try to ring Kelly. She's doing a night shift, so she must have gone to work.

All I can get is her answering machine. So I leave a message begging her to come and bail me out.

At this stage they ask me and about twenty other blokes to go into a room and take our clothes off. Then they put us in orange prison gear and give us each a cup, soap, toothbrush, toothpaste and a towel, and lead us off into the proper prison to go to bed for the night with the other prisoners.

I get thrown into a cell with this young black guy, and I ask him why he's in there and he goes, 'I'm in for public drunkenness'. I ask, 'So how long have you been in here for?' and he goes, 'I've been in here for ten days'. It turns out that he couldn't pay the fine. I say, 'Are you telling me that if I can't pay the fine I'm gonna get ten days?' He says, 'No. I got twenty days. This is my tenth day.'

Right now I'm shitting myself. If Kelly can't pay the fine for me…well I'd only just met her, why should she? Anyway at seven that night they finally release me because Kelly had come down, but it took them four hours to process everything.

I'm too scared to go out that night. I have to go back to court the following day. Kelly isn't mad, but I don't want to stay in

New Orleans after that, not with a twenty-day suspended prison sentence.

We've been emailing each other ever since. I've told her if she ever comes to Australia she can stay with me. She was lovely, she was gorgeous...that stupid cop! Ruined my whole holiday!

Tonight? I'm sorry, but...I have to go to the police station to see if I'm still missing.

Driven Crazy

Penny, 17

One fine Friday night my mum's best friend's son Johnno—who I had been set up with—picked me up to go to the movies. I hadn't seen much of Johnno since he had almost drowned my cat Bubbles in his backyard pool when we were ten. But hey, that was a long time ago and people change, right?

Johnno came and picked me up, and Mum insisted that he come in and have a cup of tea and a chat before we left. She did the usual very embarrassing, 'You've grown. I hardly recognise you. Aren't you handsome!' sort of stuff. I was surprised—Johnno *was* looking pretty cute these days. I took advantage of Mum's babbling to go and put some mascara on.

Finally Mum let us go and Johnno walked me out to his car. It was actually his parents' BMW with Johnno's P-plates on it. I hopped in nervously.

Just before we got to the cinema, we were pulled over by the police. Johnno had been swerving in and out of lanes so recklessly that the policeman thought he must be drunk and asked him to get out of the car and do a breath test.

When the policeman realised we were both sober, he asked why our car had been swerving. Johnno told the policeman that he'd been so involved in our conversation, that he'd had trouble paying attention to the road. I had to hold back a snort of disbelief. Our 'conversation' had been all about Johnno. Johnno talking about *his* job, *his* ex-girlfriend, *his* school, *his* friends and *his* family. I hadn't said anything at all.

After the movie, Johnno decided to avoid the cops by taking the long way home. He started talking about himself—again not letting me get a word in. In the process, he failed to notice a small dog walking along the side of the road. After he hit the poor thing, I screamed for Johnno to stop and turn around, but he just looked at me strangely and kept driving.

And to top it off, when we finally got to my house, he told me he'd had a really great time and asked if I wanted to go out for dinner on Sunday. I answered as calmly as I could, 'Thanks Johnno…but I just don't think that would be a good idea'.

[Original story courtesy of ivillage.com/relationships.]

Tonight? I'm sorry, but…it wouldn't be fair to the other beautiful people.

German Date

Nathan, 30

I was in the south of France and I met this gorgeous German girl called Julia (pronounced Yulia) in a club. I called her the next day and she asked me to come and meet her at the beach. I thought, 'Well, well! This could be very good.'

So I went down to the beach, and there were four young girls lying there naked. I was trying not to look, but was sort of slightly looking. As I got closer one of them jumped up and started waving her arms going, 'Nathan! Nathan! How are you?' and of course it was Julia. So over I went.

I was standing there next to these four naked girls in my board shorts with my surfboard and wondering if I should strip off, but then I started getting this huge boner. So I lay down and became a bit more at ease with the situation. In fact I really started to enjoy myself.

A bit later we got up to go for a swim. But Julia's parents happened to be about twenty metres up the beach and they proceeded to come over to us. So Julia introduced me to her mother and father, who were also completely naked. Her father Stefan borrowed my surfboard and went out for a little surf…nude!

He'd never surfed before in his life, and I was thinking, 'Pubes on my wax, there's gotta be some kind of action happening there…'

But he did proceed to pay back the favour. I had an injury from eating a baguette. You know how hard baguettes are—very crusty bread. I had cut the back of my gum, which was now inflamed. It turned out that Julia's father was a dentist and she invited me over so he could fix my tooth. This was all before we had even kissed by the way—nothing had happened yet.

So later that day I went over to their bungalow. I was lying there with my head back on three big books on their kitchen table, and who else travels with a whole dentist kit but the Germans? They'd come prepared. They had all the German sausages; they had everything in this house.

Julia's mother was the dental nurse, and they had painkillers and everything, so Julia's dad stitched me up and when I was ready to go he said, 'See ya Nathan! Take Julia with you!'

So I took Julia out with me and we were having our first kiss after her dad had just stitched my mouth up—I had this cotton thing in between my gums and I couldn't feel anything because of the painkillers. But Julia didn't seem to mind and we ended up seeing each other until she went home.

Oh and I checked my surfboard the next day—you guessed it, there were indeed several grey pubes stuck in my wax. Yeeeech. I could never look at Julia's father (or her mother) the same way again.

Tonight? I'm sorry, but…I made an appointment with a cuticle specialist.

High Rollers

Sonia, 32

So I was an Australian girl in Vegas, and I decided to go out to a bar, as you do. A few hours into the night I met this guy and it turned out that he was the son of the vice-president of a huge oil corporation, who had just died. He was about 30, and he was living at Caesars Palace and basically gambling all the time.

He was heading over to the casino to play some poker and he asked me if I wanted to come. I didn't have much money but I told him that I'd give him the $60 I had on me. If he won he could give it back to me plus some extra, and if he lost I'd just lose the money.

So I sat with him on the gaming tables for two days without a break. I remember thinking, 'He's going to inherit all this money really soon and he's going to blow it all'. So I was jinxing him—I didn't want him to win. I wanted to prove to him what it was like to lose, and he did. He just lost and lost and lost and lost.

I think it was his idea of romance—for me to be there at the gaming tables with him. And it was actually quite sexy because this guy was playing with such a lot of money and saying, 'Give me a kiss for luck'. He was entering exclusive tournaments and meanwhile I was drinking coffee, and time was ticking by…but it was Vegas and they never tell you what the time is.

Eventually up came this guy called the Major. He was about 50, and a blackjack high roller who also lived in the casino. He asked me if I'd had anything to eat and I said, 'Actually I haven't had anything to eat since yesterday morning'. And he went, 'Let me take you out to lunch because this guy's not going to leave the tables'.

So the Major took me out to lunch and he was telling about how he had two mistresses there in Vegas, and how he paid their living allowances. He said to me, 'You can stay here if you want to, I'll just set you up'. I said, 'Oh that's really, really lovely, but that's all right', but I got his name and address anyway.

I went back to the casino and found the guy. He was still playing, still throwing thousands and thousands of dollars out onto the table and still losing and losing and losing. Late that night I convinced him to leave with me. We wound up back in a tacky hotel room and I gave him a blow job or something and that was the end of the date. It had been two whole days and two nights. The next morning I was leaving Las Vegas, and the oil billionaire's son went back to work—freeing himself of his father's money. I wonder how long it took him.

Tonight? I'm sorry, but...I'm teaching my ferret to yodel.

Meet the Folks

Adam, 22

I hadn't met my new girlfriend Shelley's parents, although I knew her father was *really* protective and strict…bear in mind that I was 22 and she was 18…Anyway, we were drinking at the local pub near her house one Saturday night, way out in the suburbs. We hung out in the park and talked and whatever until a bit after 12 am. When Shelley headed home I staggered off to the train station.

The trains were listed as running every thirty minutes until like 6 am. So I waited and an hour passed…no trains…two hours…I fell asleep on the platform in the freezing cold for another hour and was woken every so often by passing freight trains, but the scheduled trains never came!

So I figured, even though I didn't have any money on me (I just had my return train ticket) I could get a cab home then one of my flatmates could let me in to get some money to pay for the cab. I approached a bunch of scary looking guys who were silently sitting around a table in the park at 4 am. They debated for about five minutes as to whether or not they should let me use their phone before eventually handing it over.

So I called my place and none of my flatmates were home! Or at least they were so dead they couldn't even hear the phone. So I wandered around again for a while trying to figure out what the hell I was going to do. Eventually I gave in and decided to call

Shelley. She was like, 'Adam, how come you didn't call me earlier!'
She told me to come around, so I stumbled my way there.

When I arrived at Shelley's house she was stealthily opening
the front door, but the family dog heard me coming and ran up
barking its head off! Every bedroom in the house opened onto
the main hallway. We stood there frozen as one by one, all of
Shelley's family stepped out of their respective doorways and
blinked at me sleepily in their pyjamas.

Shelley's dad was less than pleased (he is the only male in a
family of six). He grunted at us to 'Get some sleep', while
Shelley's mum set up the spare mattress in the living room.
Shelley got in shit loads of trouble the next day and wasn't
allowed out for two weeks.

A less than impressive way to introduce myself to her family,
methinks, but after a good old fashioned, 'what are your intentions
with my daughter?' chat I won Shelley's dad over…well almost.

*Tonight? I'm sorry, but…I'm going
through chocolate mud cake withdrawal.*

Model Behaviour

Luke, 19

O ne night I took out a friend of mine's little sister. Her name was Chrissie and she was 17 and a model. Drop dead gorgeous. We went to the movies and she let me hold her hand and put my arm around her. Afterwards she said, 'Let's go to the Oaks for a drink'. The Oaks is one of my favourite hangouts, so I said, 'Cool, let's go!'

Not long after we got there, some old friends of mine saw us and came over to say hi. I asked them to join us, and introduced them all to Chrissie.

Now one of my friends is one of those people you just can't help loving, she's a legend. But unfortunately she is, in a word, obese. She sat down next to me and we started to chat.

Suddenly Chrissie started telling the rudest fat jokes you have ever heard!

'She's so fat she's got her own postcode.'

'She's so fat when she swims in the ocean blue whales come up to her and sing "We are family".'

Nobody laughed. My friend went bright red and just stared at Chrissie in shock. I couldn't believe it and said, 'Stop it Chrissie!' but she just got louder and louder and the jokes got worse and worse.

'She's so fat that when she has sex she has to give directions!'

After a few minutes of this behaviour, I stood up and asked if anyone wanted to go to another bar that had a really good band playing that night. Everyone agreed and when Chrissie grabbed her bag, I looked her in the eyes and said, 'Sorry, Chrissie but you're not invited. Nobody treats my friends like that.'

Two tables that were close enough to hear Chrissie's jokes cheered us as we left her sitting there open-mouthed over being dumped for a fat chick.

Tonight? I'm sorry, but...I'm being deported.

Baby Love

Oliver, 22

I had just broken up with my girlfriend of three years, and I was miserable. So I stupidly agreed to a blind date with my flatmate's girlfriend's cousin. On the night of the date I nervously rang her doorbell. A girl who looked no older than 13 answered the door. I asked for Bobbi, she said, 'That's me'. I was speechless. I asked her age and she said 17. She was wearing a baggy pink tracksuit, and had braces and pigtails.

I didn't want to disappoint my flatmate so I met Bobbi's parents, who were freaks. They told me 'Baby Bobbi' needed to be in by 9.30, and it was 7.

I took her to a cafe, where she ordered a meal and ate half of it. I asked her what she liked to do and she said, 'Play with my Barbies, and my dollies'. So we went to get a video, and guess what she chose— *The Little Mermaid* and *Finding Nemo*. So for the rest of the evening Bobbi and her parents and I watched *The Little Mermaid* and *Finding Nemo*. I never called Baby Bobbi again.

Tonight? I'm sorry but I have to study for a blood test.

Mr Too Cool

Amelia, 20

This was when I lived in Brisbane. I hated this guy the first time I met him and he hated me because I was dealing drugs at the time. He called me the Pharmacist. I called him Mr Too Cool. He really had tickets on himself—he was very good-looking, stylish and extremely well-toned. He had girls falling all over him, but I wasn't impressed. I was 18, I'd just broken up from an intense, year-long relationship and I just wanted to have fun.

He took me out on this date. We went to dinner then we went to the pub. We'd had two drinks when he started to wig out and get nervous. He kept checking his watch, which struck me as odd as he was the one who suggested going for beers after dinner.

Finally I said, 'Look, do you have to get home?' He was like, 'No, no, no, it's fine', but he kept looking at his watch so I asked him again, 'What's wrong?' He started to get aggressive and said, 'Look Amelia, it's really late'. It was like 10 pm, not late at all. I went, 'Whoa, back the fuck up, what's going on?'

Suddenly he started talking about his dad and how he was in the police force. He choked up a bit then started crying. I took him outside and he went from this tall coolio, to sitting on the bonnet of the car hunched over, sobbing his heart out.

I thought his dad must beat him up or something like that, but no—it was just that he was going to be late getting the car back. He was sitting there crying and it was getting later and later. I looked at him and I said, 'It's alright, it's okay. Don't worry we'll get the car home', and I gave him advice on how to talk to his dad.

After that night was over, I thought, 'He's piss weak, this is never going to work'. But then I did some research and found out that he was always going from one girl to the next—bailing out on dates and never, ever sleeping with them. And the way he always interacted with women—it was just so showy: 'Look how many girls I've had!' But being with him I could see that he hadn't really had much experience at all.

I think he had huge issues with his policeman dad and I think it was because he was gay. I felt kind of sorry for him. We didn't date again, we didn't even talk to each other after that, so I don't know if he ever worked up the guts to come out and stop putting himself through the horribly arduous torture of dating girls.

Tonight? I'm sorry, but...I have to go to my Kamahl Fan Club meeting.

Karaoke Madness

Dan, 27

I had just worked up the guts to ask out this girl from work, and we had decided on a karaoke bar downtown. Dinner was great, and then the karaoke started. Let's just say I didn't know she was such a fan. She quickly put in a few requests to do some songs, and I actually got sort of turned on by the fact that she was so confident about herself. The first two singers were great, and then it was her turn.

She quickly grabbed the microphone and began this outburst of yelping and whining, 'singing' along with Madonna's 'Like a Virgin'. I just about died laughing, but then I realised that this was not a joke; she really sang like this. Then she started dancing really badly onstage and beckoned for me to join her. Of course, I acted like I had no idea who she was.

I was so embarrassed to be seen with her that I left as soon as she turned around to get ready for her next song.

Tonight? I'm sorry but...I'm getting married tonight.

Freaks and Weirdos

The world is full of individuals, and some are just a bit more individual than others. These poor souls have a rough time in the dating world. So rest assured, you are not the only person who has attracted a freak or two…they're out there.

Age 13 My worst date was a really bad dresser—she was wearing tracksuit pants and ugh boots. She had not brushed her teeth that morning. We played spin the egg since we didn't have a bottle. She did not know how to kiss. She kissed like a dog and she bit my lip.

Age 15 This guy and me were on a blind date. We were watching *Bambi*!! He said he didn't have anything else, so I just gave in, thinking that we wouldn't spend much time *watching* the movie. I mean we were in his bedroom, on his bed. Well, anyway, during the part where Bambi's mum dies he started *sobbing*!! He kept saying, 'Life is sooo unfair' and 'Why did she have to die?' I started laughing out loud—I thought he was joking! But then he ran outside and started bawling about how mean people were to him. I followed him outside and said I was sorry. Then he said he needed to call his mum for a moment, please. After that I told him I had to leave and he tried to kiss me. I told him that I wasn't interested, so would he please not kiss me. Then his face turned red and he started to cry again. I was out of there in a flash!

Age 21 I had been dating this guy (an opera singer I had known for a year) for about a week when we decided to sleep together. I had always thought that women were the ones who make noise, but after this experience I realised I was wrong. We were out on a date and decided to go home early, but when we pulled into my driveway, my parents' car was there. Not wanting to wait for another chance, we decided to park the car around the back and just do it there. After about five minutes of foreplay we got down to business—and he started to sing during sex. It wasn't soft singing, either; it was as loud as you could imagine. Dogs started barking, and I was trying to quieten him down. My parents, hearing the disturbance, came out and saw us doing it. The worst part was that they just stood there in disbelief, not saying a word. It was the worst night of my life.

Age 24 When my date picked me up, I noticed an intriguing briefcase sandwiched between the seats in his car. I wondered about it because he was a bus driver. What could he possibly need a business briefcase for? Religious work? Travel? Then he said, 'You know, we don't have to go to the movies. We could get to know each other better if we got a hotel room.' Stunned, I said, 'No. I don't want to rush into anything. I like to take it slow.' 'But I know you're wondering what's in here', he teased and put the briefcase on my lap. Even though I started to explain it was really none of my business and I would just rather go to the movies, he opened that baby up. It was filled with sex toys, gel, massage oil and things I couldn't even guess the use of! I opened the car door and got the hell out of there.

[Original story courtesy of ivillage.com/relationships.]

Age 28 My friend set me up with this guy that she thought I would really click with. When he showed up at my house, I thought he was pretty cute. The date started out fine…until I worked out where we were going. He took me to a strip club and even ordered a lap dance! Then he said he had a surprise for me. The next thing I knew I was being dragged onto the stage by two naked women. I was furious! Then when I got off the stage he was mad that I didn't strip, and then he started touching my breasts. Can we say arsehole? I walked home.

Age 30 I met a man who introduced himself as a computer professional—he was intelligent, well-dressed and attractive. We decided to meet at a local restaurant for dinner. However, the conversation started to lag. I found myself trying to fill in the obvious gaps with small talk, but I was having better luck speaking to the waiter! When I turned the subject to movies, he became animated, telling me about his love for the films *Star Wars*, *Star Trek* and so on. Finally I thought we were back on track. But the more he talked, the more hyper he became. His voice was getting higher and higher and louder and louder. I noticed that other diners were having difficulty concentrating on their own conversations. Just when I thought things couldn't get any worse, out of the blue (and in an especially high-pitched tone), he blurted, 'Do you like porno?' Everyone stopped and stared in our direction. I shook my head 'no' and tried to bury myself in my salad. He tried to regain his composure and then mumbled, 'I don't like porno either'. I didn't go out with him again.

Age 31 I had just met this girl at the gym, and I asked her out on a date. She was hot and always wore a pink leotard when she was working out. She looked great in it; but still, it kind of bothered me for some reason. So I picked her up for our night on the town, and she was wearing that same pink leotard with a denim jacket! I was shocked, and as she opened the car door to get in, I promptly told her I had forgotten something at my house and would be right back. I never went back to get her. I even changed the times when I go to the gym.

Age 33 I met this girl on the Internet. She seemed really nice—a bit too shy, maybe, and pretty self-conscious. We hung out at my house a couple of times, and she told me that somehow she had lost her teeth, and that she'd had new ones made. Well, I tried not to be too shallow; if she hadn't told me, I wouldn't have known. So I agreed to go out with her on a real date. Well, I picked her up, and we decided to go out and have steak. Everything was going fine until I looked up and saw that she had taken her teeth out. I was so embarrassed. She looked like a 70-year-old woman! Then she proceeded to try to hold my hand and tell me how nice I looked. I just wanted to crawl under the table and hide. I had lost my appetite and was praying that she would put them back in quickly. Finally, after she was completely finished eating, she put them back in and we left. We were supposed to go out to dinner the next day, but I cancelled because I was 'sick'. I don't think I could ever sit down in front of her for a meal again.

Age 34 When my date picked me up, he looked suave and handsome in his cargo pants and a sports jacket. But early in the evening, odd things started happening. First, it was unbelievably hot. Even though we were both sweating, he wouldn't take his jacket off. Then, after we were finished eating, he scooped some crumbs off his plate into a napkin and put them in his pocket. When we got back to his car, I found out why he wouldn't take the jacket off. He had a little pet mouse inside one of the pockets! Just as we both sat down in the car, he started feeding him the crumbs. This was one fuzzy little third wheel that I could do without!

Age 42 I have four weirdos for you:

1. The man who claimed his sense of humour was his greatest asset and demonstrated it by doing Groucho Marx imitations all through dinner at a fancy restaurant.

2. The man who said he saw a 'daddy' when he looked in the mirror and asked (on the first and only date) if I was ovulating.

3. The man who demanded a list of the 'specific skills and strengths' that I could bring to a relationship, as well as an analysis of the 'self-destructive patterns' that caused my divorce.

4. The man whose first words were 'I'm sorry, I've got to concentrate on getting well tonight', and who spent most of the evening with a Vicks inhaler up his nose.

Playing Hard Ball

Kelly, 36

This is about Costa, a Greek boy with a big dick, who I met while showing him a property. He calls me Mrs Robinson, because I seduced him, I went after him like you wouldn't believe. He's 31 and I'm 36, but I don't look it. I'm lucky.

I got him into my work; I got him in on a huge deal on a golf course. The energy across the boardroom table was just sizzling. He sent me a text afterwards saying, 'So that boardroom table was calling you and me…'

We had been seeing each other for a little while but things weren't going too well and I sent him a text message that said, 'Well, you know it's three strikes Costa, what's the story?' He goes, 'Yooooou're out!' On text! We broke up on SMS, can you believe it?

He goes, 'Sorry kid, it's just that I'm commitment phobic'. Yeah, how condescending is that? The fucking ego! Big dicks, big egos, little minds—Sydney men! So I'm like, 'fuck you!' He hurt me though 'cause I really liked him—Gemini, intelligent, cute, owned property, engineer…arsehole.

Anyway, a few weeks later he emailed me, 'How you doin'?' I sent back a message saying, 'I'm okay, what do you want?' He said, 'I assume you're looking as gorgeous as ever…' and I'm like, 'Yeah, and?' So we started to email again and we met up for casual sex. This happened about three times, and then…

51

It was a full moon, and I'd been out to a cocktail evening. What can I say? These cocktails were the best leg openers. They were made from an illegally imported liqueur with hallucinogenic properties; you don't have too much of it.

It had been a while so I sent Costa a text message to say I was coming over. I dressed in my super-high black stilettos and black lingerie and my beautiful, long cashmere cream coat, black gloves and a black scarf. I got a cab over there and we, hmmm, had a *fun* time.

Then we were lying in bed and Costa said, 'Well thanks for coming over, can I call you a cab?' I turned to him and said, 'What?' He said, 'It's just a principle, isn't it, for you? You have to stay the night.' I had never been asked to leave a boy's bed in my life. I just felt every hair on my body stand on end. My face went red, my teeth clenched, my knuckles went white. I thought, 'You bastard!'

And he said, 'Here, here's the phone'. I was completely lost for words. At last I said, 'The least you could do is call a cab for me, and make it a Silver Service'. I put my cashmere coat and gloves back on (I was still wearing my stilettos), informed him that he would never see me again, and out I went.

And here's the double clincher—I sent him a text the next day saying, 'Bad luck that you treated me that way, you lose out not only personally but professionally'. I cut him out of the golf course deal.

He still emails me but I haven't seen him since. Who knows, I might need him again one day. Some guys you keep on the books for just one reason, because they are no good for anything else.

Tonight? I'm sorry, but…I'm converting my calendar from Julian to Gregorian.

Undercover Agent

Emma, 29

I dated a really nice man for about three months. He was tall and handsome and spoke with an Italian accent that made me melt. I was living a dream—until one night when he came over to pick me up for dinner. Something about him was different. He had a 'cat that ate the canary' look on his face. We settled down on the couch with glasses of wine, and he said, 'I have been a *bad boy*'.

I thought to myself, 'No, he can't mean what I think he means'. So I asked him what he was talking about. Wow, was I in for the shock of my life! He said, 'I've been wearing these all day' and stood up, dropped his pants and revealed a garter belt, stockings and a G-string! To top things off, he then said, 'I need to be *spanked*'. I was laughing so hard I couldn't get the door open fast enough for him to leave!

Tonight? I'm sorry, but...I don't want to leave my comfort zone.

Senior Squabbles

Nellie, 66

I am 66 years old and a widow; I lost my husband about ten years ago from a heart attack. I have to admit that going on a date at my age was quite an experience. I had recently met a man at the local greengrocer, and we decided to spend some time together. He invited me to join him for a picnic and to go fishing. When I arrived at the park, I was delighted to find that he had thoughtfully prepared an afternoon for the two of us.

Things were going very well until our fishing expedition turned sour. It had been hours since either of us had caught anything, and time was just ticking away. So I decided that I would be nice and start up a conversation about the weather. He responded by yelling at me because I was disturbing the fish and the wildlife, and told me to shut up. I got very offended by his comment and decided to leave.

He didn't care.

He was so occupied with his pole in the water that he didn't even try to stop me.

Harvey, 58

'm no spring chicken, at 58, and I'm not a movie star look-alike—but I'm not ugly, either. So sometimes I will find a lady who is interested in dinner or sharing some time together fishing, my favourite outdoor activity.

One woman whom I met while shopping seemed genuinely interested in joining me for an afternoon of fishing, so we made a date to do just that. What happened was a complete disaster. She should have said that what she really likes about fishing with someone is having a captive audience for her endless monologue.

After an hour of nonstop drivel delivered at the speed of an auctioneer, she let me interrupt her long enough to ask if she would mind not talking for a minute, so I could hear a waterbird sing.

The reaction was as if I had insulted her mother: instant hostility. She left in a huff, talking all the while of my brutish behaviour. It was the worst match of two people that you can imagine. I'm sure she felt the same.

Tonight? I'm sorry, but...I've come down with a really horrible case of something or other.

The Smoocher

Angela, 43

I met a guy online who I thought was really nice. We started to talk on the phone and decided to meet one night. He was always telling me that he was going to be the best kisser I'd ever had because all his ex-girlfriends told him what a great 'smoocher' he was. He had a really nice voice, so I pictured someone tall, with blond hair and an athletic body (he told me that he ran every morning).

I got to the bar first and ordered a drink. About ten minutes later, a short, dumpy blond guy (picture a garden gnome without the beard) walked in and came right up to me. I pretended to be totally into him.

He bought the dinner and drinks and kept talking about how pretty I was and what a great time we were going to have dating. I told him it was really getting late and that I had to go. He offered to walk me out. When we got to my car, I turned to give him a hug—and immediately he jammed his tongue into my mouth—and left it there! He didn't move his tongue at all! I finally pushed him off and got into my car and drove away. I would like to find all the girls who told him that he was a great kisser, because it was the worst kiss of my life!

Tonight? I'm sorry, but...I have to check the use-by-dates of the food in my fridge.

Skinny Dipping

Damien, 19

I was taking this girl Katie from my uni out for our second date. The first time we went out it was just to the uni bar so I wanted this to be special. It was a really warm evening and I thought, what could be more romantic than a walk along the beach followed by a late night picnic under the stars? I begged Dad to lend me his car. He said, 'Get it back by eleven'.

I picked Katie up and we drove down to the beach. I parked at the far end and took out my backpack. I had a blanket with me and a nice bottle of wine. We headed up to the park on the headland where I found us a secluded place on the cliffs.

I spread out the blanket and we opened the wine. It was incredibly romantic. We drank the whole thing. Katie and I started kissing, and before long we were rolling around with half our clothes off. Then she said, 'Lets go skinny dipping!'

We ran down the hill. The beach was pretty deserted and dark, so no-one would see us. We stripped off and jumped into the water and swam around for a while. Katie wrapped her legs around me and we started pashing again. I was getting so into it I didn't notice that we'd drifted down the beach a bit.

We ran nude up the beach to where our stuff was but we couldn't find it. I think someone must have nicked our clothes while we were swimming. Anyway we were standing there shivering and naked on the beach and our clothes were gone and there was no-one in sight so we just ran back up the hill.

Luckily the backpack was still there with Dad's car keys in it! We put the blanket around us both anyway and ran back down to the car, pissing ourselves laughing. When we got to the car we were both saturated and covered in dirt and sand, and my Dad's car had a tan leather interior.

Katie told me there was no way she could go home like that so I offered to take her to my house so she could have a shower and borrow some clothes. I was so scared that the cops would pull us over that I drove the really long way. I parked as quietly as I could and we went around the back.

But we walked into the kitchen and there were my parents! They were cleaning up after dinner—it was only 9.30! We opened the door and just stood there—Katie in the blanket and me totally nude. Mum and Dad looked up and just stared. Katie tried to hide behind me and I had to grab a plate to cover myself. My parents hadn't seen me naked since I was 12 years old!

Mum was just laughing as I introduced them, but Dad wasn't. In the end Mum lent Katie some clothes and Dad drove her home. When he came back I copped it for the filthy car and was banned from driving it for a month. Katie and I are still very happily together, but we try to keep the public nudity to a minimum!

Tonight? I'm sorry, but...I have to fulfil my potential.

The Reluctant Spunk

Michael, 30

While online one day, I ran into a girl called Shelley with whom I had gone to high school. I found out she was now back at home, living with her parents. Eventually we decided to go out for dinner and it turned out to be one of the most embarrassing dates I've ever had.

Shelley's well-endowed cousin answered the door and she was wearing a white T-shirt over a very revealing bra. I walked in and was greeted by Shelley, her mum, and the family dog. As I entered the room, the dog immediately walked up to me and started sniffing between my legs as everyone looked on. I asked whether the dog was a female or male, and Shelley replied, 'Female'. At that moment, the dog turned around, presenting its tail as if it were expecting me to bonk it!

Everyone laughed, and I asked Shelley if she was ready to go. We went out for dinner and then the movies, but the conversation went nowhere because I could not get the eerie thought out of my mind that someone must have done the dog before!

After the movie, I was preparing to drive Shelley home when she offered to head over to my place. 'No, maybe some other time', I politely declined. To which she replied, 'Why not? You're a spunk; even my dog thought so!'

Tonight? I'm sorry but...I'm giving blood.

Who's Charlie?

Crystal, 30

his is about a date that my boyfriend had…without me. I was new to Sydney, but I'd been dating this guy for three months, and I let him have the key for the first time ever to stay in my place while I was away on an overnight trip (I'm a flight attendant).

I came home and found two champagne glasses in the sink. I thought, 'Okay, maybe he had a friend over'. But then I went into the bedroom and found long black hairs on the white sheets. I went straight back out to the glasses and I just knew there was gonna be lipstick on the glass. There was. And you know how your heart just falls out of your chest? I hate that feeling.

So then I called him and he denied that he'd had anyone over. I finally just said 'There are black hairs in the bed and lipstick on the glass, what did you do?' So then he finally admitted it and told me that this girl Amber was in the house but nothing happened.

I hung up on him, and then he got in his car and rang me to say he was coming over. I asked him who Amber was and he told me I'd met her before and that she was a friend of his.

They'd run into each other at a bar in the city and come back to my house to party. Amber had slept in my bed and he'd slept on the couch—that's what he told me, anyway.

I remembered that I had met Amber once at a party. And that one day he had told me he was going to Amber's to pick up

Charlie...I'd assumed Charlie was a boy. Then it all came together. Obviously Charlie was cocaine. What an idiot I was.

So Amber was his drug dealer. But you see, I'd never been around drugs before. Now it was obvious. God I was an idiot!

His friends had all assumed that I was on it too, they just went, 'She's blonde, skinny and fun, she must be on coke'. When I told them how shocked I was they said, 'You mean you're like that without drugs?'

So he'd been to this bar, met this slut, taken her back to my place and snorted coke on my dining room table and slept with her in my bed. That was a great welcome home, that one!

I had the house feng shuied afterwards, and the feng shui lady told me to give the sheets away.

Tonight? I'm sorry but...The Sound of Music is on tonight.

Smooth Dick

Rochelle, 28

I was heading out on a date with this guy Travis that I had met the night before. He had VIP tickets to see a hot DJ from the UK who was playing at this huge nightclub in the city. I thought Travis was cute and funny, from what I could remember of the night before, but we had met in a club when I was off my face, so you know, he'd *seemed* cute.

He picked me up and we caught a taxi to the club. He was okay looking after all, and he was paying for everything. Half an hour after getting into the club we'd had two drinks but the conversation was going nowhere, the UK DJ wasn't due to play for another hour and Travis didn't want to dance. I thought, 'This guy is really boring'.

I came to the conclusion that the only way to survive such a boring night was to drink more alcohol. So I had a few more drinks and the evening started to improve a bit. The DJ was playing some great tracks and I was getting really into the music—Travis even seemed cuter. Finally we hit the floor and started to dance. Travis could shake it pretty well after all, and the music was fantastic.

We went and sat back down and Travis started fondling me. I knew it was the alcohol, but I thought, 'Maybe I'll take you home—you're cute, so you know, maybe'.

Anyway, while we were fumbling he suddenly looked me in the

eyes and said, 'I've got a smooth dick'. I thought I'd heard him wrong. I said, 'What?' And he shouted in my ear, 'I've got a smooooth dick!'

I guess from the look he gave me he was expecting me to say, 'Ooh yeah, let's go now, 'cause I just love smooth dicks!'

I was shocked, I was like, 'I'm sorry?' In my mind I was wondering, 'Is that meant to turn me on? God—what an idiot!'

Anyway, needless to say I took control of the situation, and we headed off in a taxi home. And it was smooth. It was as smooth and it was about as thin and pointy as a pencil. C'est la vie.

I didn't see Travis again but I don't feel sorry for him—he's obviously quite happy with his lot.

Tonight? I'm sorry, but...I have to bleach my hare.

Gender Benders

When what you see is not necessarily what you're gonna get…

Age 23 When Jason, a guy I met online, asked me out, I suggested we each bring a friend along in order to make everyone feel more comfortable. Jason brought a gorgeous guy who was tall and blonde with blue eyes—my friend was very pleased! As for me, I was confused. Jason was strange-looking and awkward. I couldn't figure out what it was that was weird though. He just seemed odd. As soon as we had a minute alone, my friend filled me in on the secret. Her date had told her that Jason was really a woman! I politely declined to see 'Jason' again, but my friend and 'his' friend dated for a while.

Age 26 One day I was going to get my usual morning cafe latte. As I was ordering, I noticed this really hot guy staring at me from a few tables away. After about ten minutes he came over to my table and asked if I would like to go out with him that night. I was kind of hesitating, but I gave him my phone number, and we made plans to go out that evening. He invited me over for dinner and the main course was takeaway McDonald's! I was already annoyed, and then he started to put the moves on me. Soon enough he had ripped off all of his clothes. In complete shock I stared downward to get a look at his package. That's how I found out that he was not really a he but a she! I later found out that he was a transsexual. His surgery to become a full male was the next week. I am still trying to get over that one!

Age 27 There was this girl in my yoga class who I knew had a thing for me, because she always seemed to be positioned right behind me; and I often caught her staring at my behind. Anyway, I finally asked her to go on a date, and she happily agreed. We went to a concert and had dinner afterward; everything seemed great. Luckily, that particular night my flatmates weren't home, so I had the house to myself. My date seemed really aroused when I asked her to come in for a while to have a drink. Things went along as planned, and we started making out heavily. She stripped off all my clothes and became extremely kinky, doing cool things like biting my nipples. I hastily started to undress my partner, and to my horrified surprise, she had *both* pieces of equipment! I grabbed my clothing and ran out of my house, leaving her naked in my bedroom.

Age 30 It's amazing how good some guys look in make-up and heels. Steven Tyler of Aerosmith sings about it in 'Dude Looks like a Lady' and I found out about it first-hand when I went out to a bar in London. I was feeling lucky and I was seeing some beautiful ladies. Then I spotted this incredible creature. She was tall, really built and more than willing to do anything I had in mind. The only problem was, when we got back to my place I found out that she was really a he—a very well endowed he and definitely the wrong gender for me. It was really awkward, but we talked about it and eventually ended up having a laugh about it.

The Drooler

Tania, 14

I was dating this guy that I had been like madly in love with ever since I was 9, and when we started going out it was like a dream come true…until it came to an awful end.

We'll call this guy 'D'. D has dark brown hair and a chocolate coloured birthmark on his neck and he surfs and plays football. He is also very funny and smart and his handwriting is perfect. All the girls love him and he has always, *always* had a girlfriend.

The year we started high school D moved to my street. Can you believe it? He rode past my house on his bike with a surfboard under one arm at least eight times per weekend.

On the school bus one afternoon, D told me that he knew I had a yellow bikini. I asked him how he knew that. He said that my best friend told him. He went, 'You in a bikini Tania? I mean, Sally Adams, okay, she has boobs…but *you*? You are a *surfboard*!' and he laughed his head off.

But that was last year. On the bus on the way home a few weeks ago, I heard D's friend from the year above us (the best surfer in the school) talking to D. He was saying, 'That girl Tania has got it *bad* for you mate, she's always staring at ya'. I was just panicking because I knew D would never like me back.

The next day D came up to me in the schoolyard at lunchtime. He invited me over to his house that night to just hang out and watch TV. My best friend and I went into the girls toilets and screamed. I was so happy. On the school bus D and I sat next to each other and he held my hand so everyone in the bus knew that we were going out. I was really nervous because soon we were going to be alone together.

D's Mum and Dad were really cool—they always wore tracksuits and did lots of sport too. We had spaghetti for dinner and cordial, which I am normally not allowed to drink, and we were allowed to watch TV at the same time. When we had finished eating dinner we went down to D's rumpus room to have a look at his surfboard. We were sitting there on the couch wrestling and just having fun till he leaned over and kissed me. Well I loved him so much I just couldn't help myself, so I kissed him back…and before I knew it, he was lying on top of me. I'm not making this up…*we were practically having sex with all our clothes on!*

Well, I didn't want to be mean and just push him off so we kept on kissing until he finally got off me. When I sat up I realised I had spit running down my chin—D had slobbered all over my face! It was so disgusting, as soon as he wasn't looking I wiped the spit off with my T-shirt. I mean it was literally on my cheeks and nose and everything!

Well, thank God that my mum came to pick me up about fifteen minutes later so I didn't have to sit there and look at him for long.

After that night, we stopped talking at the bus stop and on the bus but it seems like I see him around more than ever. To make it even worse, I told my best friend about the slobber and she spread it around the whole school and the poor guy can't get a girlfriend now! Damn, what a total waste of hotness. I hope I never have to go through anything like that again!

Tonight? I'm sorry, but…my yucca plant is feeling yucky.

The Horse Handler

Lachlan, 28

This girl used to work in a cocktail bar and her name was Bronwyn. She was going out with someone but I kept calling out, 'Bronwyn, I think I love you!' and stuff like that over the bar while she was working. Eventually she broke up with her boyfriend and agreed to go for a drink with me.

On the first date I found out that her family had a horse husbandry farm and I told her that I'd always wanted to live in the country and I would love to learn how to ride horses. She had to go down there to work that weekend, and she invited me to go with her. So I went.

The farm was two hours south of Sydney and really massive and super nice. It was a bit uncomfortable because I didn't really know Bronwyn very well, and her family was quite posh.

It was pissing down with rain that day but we went off to this small paddock and Bronwyn showed me how to ride. I got on one of her horses, but the horse didn't like me on its back and it butted me off. I got thrown into the air and landed on my back in the mud. My foot got stuck in the stirrup but the horse kept running and I was dragged around and around in the mud.

I was really freaking out. When the horse finally stopped I stood up quickly, covered in mud from head to toe, and fell back onto the fence, which was one of those electric fences. I got electrocuted on the fence, and then I got thrown forward and landed face first in the mud again.

This all happened within two hours of my getting there. So I went inside and recovered for a couple of hours. I wasn't really getting along that well with Bronwyn or her family either—I felt uncomfortable and I was tired and crabby.

Later in the afternoon we went back to mate the horses. The stallion had like this massive dong, and they let him into the same paddock as the mare, and the stallion mounted the mare. This was pretty embarrassing and intimidating for me already, but to make it all happen properly—because people pay money for the mare to be impregnated—Bronwyn had to grab the dong and stick it into the mare. So I just stood there watching in horror as she grabbed this massive red thing and stuck it in this horse, it completely freaked me out. The whole experience just freaked me out.

Anyway I remember going to bed pretty early that night and just waking up in the morning and taking off pretty early back to the city. I never went out with Bronwyn again.

Tonight? I'm sorry, but...my chocolate-appreciation class meets that night.

The Non-Green Eater

Catherine, 27

had been using one of those online dating sites and wasn't having much luck. I'd met 87 guys with 312 different disorders, from, 'My mother comes over everyday to clean my sheets', to 'I don't eat anything green'; and of course, the dreaded 'I forgot I was 48 years old—I thought I was 32!'

So, here I was having coffee with a seemingly charming date. His emails were funny, he had a normal job, he was well educated, but then…utter disaster! 'I don't eat anything green', he said. I thought to myself, 'How could I have found yet another non-green eater? Was there a fiasco in 1980 that I missed involving lettuce attacking young children?' I asked him, 'Nothing green? No lettuce? Not even a cucumber? A lime? A pea?' 'Nothing green!'

I had assumed at this point that the joke was on me. This man must have been a friend of the other non-green eater, whom I had dumped due to his disgust at my food colour nonchalance. There are only so many times you can hear, 'Are you really going to eat that hamburger with *pickles* and (gasp) *lettuce*?'

Despite my paranoia I continued the conversation as normally as possible. As we were talking, he dropped the name of a girl I had gone to high school with. Three rounds of coffee later we said our goodbyes and discussed another date. He really wasn't so bad, assuming I wasn't the brunt of a joke. We were yet to have a meal, but the situation alone made him worthy of another date in my eyes.

I rushed home and called the old school friend he had talked about. We chatted and caught up. Then I mentioned my reason for calling. I explained that I had been on a blind date and needed to verify if she, in fact, knew this man and could substantiate whether or not he ate green food. So I said his name. Which she followed with a long pause.

Did she not know him? If she did know him, was she going to break the truth to me—that he *did* indulge in all things leafy and green? Finally, an answer: 'Oh, I know him, and he doesn't eat anything green'. (Phew.) 'But, I know him because I live with him. He's my boyfriend!'

Some good did come of this bizarre fiasco, as I was reconnected with an old friend. She dumped that cheating bastard (after his laughable 'take me back!' whimpering). So all's well that ends well in the land of green eaters.

Tonight? I'm sorry, but...I never go out on days that end in 'y'.

The Pleather Jacket

Scott, 35

When I was 11 years old I had a crush on the prettiest girl in the class, Susannah Briggs. I asked her to come to the movies with me one Saturday afternoon and she said yes. My mother bought me a new jacket for the occasion. It was black and shiny and looked like leather but it was really plastic—it was pleather.

I took the train to the station and waited on the platform for Susannah. I was feeling very cool and confident in my new jacket. Suddenly Susannah's best friend Kelly appeared. She came up to me and said, 'I'm sorry to have to tell you like this Scott, but Susannah can't make it today'.

She watched my face fall, and before I could ask any questions she took off. Then I saw Susannah and about six girls from my class jump out from behind a pillar and run off laughing down the platform. At the bottom of the stairs Susannah and Kelly stopped and turned to me. Susannah took one look in my direction and burst out laughing again. Kelly bit her lip and shrugged her shoulders at me, pushing Susannah up the stairs.

Two days later at school, those girls had spread it around that 'Scott Leary has a pleather jacket'. I was utterly mortified and stayed home sick for a week.

When my mother finally asked me why I was moping about so much I told her. For my birthday two weeks later she bought me a real leather jacket. I wore it to the school dance that Friday. Susannah pointed at me and laughed, thinking I had worn my pleather jacket to the dance. Then I showed a few people the label, and everyone realised that Susannah Briggs had been telling stories.

Kelly came up to me and asked me to dance, and we ended up going out together.

Tonight? I'm sorry, but...I just picked up a book called Glue in Many Lands and I can't put it down.

The Plumber

Simone, 26

I was at the end of a four-year relationship when I met this guy. I used to cut his hair actually and one day he asked me out. He said he wanted to take me to a revolving restaurant at the top of one of the tallest buildings in the city for Valentine's Day. I thought, 'Woah that's a bit intense for a first date!' But I said, 'Yeah I'll go to dinner with you, but not on Valentine's Day'.

He called me up a week later and said, 'So do you want to go out?' Then he suggested that we go for drinks at his local RSL club. I thought, 'Oh, well that's a far cry from dinner in a five-star restaurant, but I am a down-to-earth girl, I'll go'.

He asked me how I was getting there and when I said that I would probably drive he said, 'Cool, can you pick me up?'

He lived nowhere near me—he was two suburbs away in the opposite direction from the club—but I went to pick him up. I rolled up and he was standing out the front of his house drinking a beer, and he had his friend there checking me out. He obviously lived at home, because his mother was also sticking her head out of the window staring at me. So he got in the car, and he had his Hawaiian shirt open and he was very, very hairy.

We got to the RSL and he asked me if I wanted a drink. We went up to the bar and I ordered a vodka, and he ordered a soft drink. He paid for his drink and stepped away from the bar. It was one vodka! How much was I gonna drink? I was driving!

I paid for my vodka and we sat down. When we finished our drinks he asked me if I wanted another one. I said yes, thinking this time he would surely pay, but the same thing happened. After that drink I said, 'Look I think I'm gonna go'.

He said, 'No, no, don't go—stay! I'll buy you a drink!' Same thing happened and I told him again that I was leaving.

He forced me to sit back down, and started to tell me how much we had in common because he was a plumber and I'm a hairdresser and he got the hair out from blocked drains. Once again I said, 'I'm going to go home now'.

But he still wouldn't let me go. He said, 'Why don't we go for a walk to the beach?' and I told him I hated the beach. He suggested a walk on the grass and I told him I hated the grass. He said, 'That's okay that you hate it'. I said, 'Will you stop agreeing with me? I just want to go home!'

At this point I was walking out to my car and he was running after me shouting, 'Can I call you? Can I call you?' I started to drive off, but there he was running along beside me, knocking on the window. So I drove him home, and the whole way he was asking me when he was going to see me again.

When we got to his house he refused to get out of the car. So I started honking. I just put my hand on the horn and kept it there until he got out.

He kept calling me and calling me and asking me out and I kept refusing him. Eventually he accepted my answer, but he got the last word in by playing the song, 'You're a bitch!' on my answering machine.

Tonight? I'm sorry, but...I have to condition/perm/curl/tease my hair.

The Reality TV Star

Amy, 25

I went on a date once with a reality TV star (RTVS). I had watched every second of the whole series so I felt that I knew him intimately. I had watched him break down over a cup of coffee, pick his nose, chase a well-endowed blonde commerce student; I had even seen him naked. I had gushily informed him of this when I introduced myself to him a week earlier. It seemed I wasn't the first girl to point out his public nudity. 'I'm so over it', he said.

Since it was a text messaged date invitation, I brought my flat-mate to the bar. We were having a laugh because it was getting late and I was going through the seven stages of grief: Shock—he's not coming! Denial—I'm having a great time anyway; Bargaining—maybe I got the time wrong; Fear—I am deluded, this wasn't a date and he's going to show up in an hour with three chicks! Anger—who the hell text messages a girl to ask them out anyway?! Despair—look at me I am so desperate I said yes to a text date, now I'm pissed in the middle of the week with my flatmate; and Acceptance—that's cool, that's funny. Maybe I should really take a look at the guys I'm dating…when in walked the RTVS himself. He had brought his brother.

The brother was really funny—my flatmate and he got along instantly. Unfortunately I wasn't getting very far with my date. We were both trying to be witty, but I had been to the gym and was dehydrated so the champagne went straight to my head. I think I was sloshing it on my pants as I talked myself up. The RTVS was wearing a shirt he'd worn a lot on the show.

We all decided to go to this huge, seedy bar where you bump into the entire world. We walked in and lo and behold all these people came swarming up to the RTVS. His friendliness had been very endearing on the show, and now he was talking to every single random punter; which was okay because some of them were really cute guys. At one point he was asked if I was his girlfriend and he said yes.

I bought a round for the lads and talked to the fans of the RTVS for a while—all about the RTVS and how nice he was and how admirable it was that he didn't sleep with the well-endowed, blonde commerce student. At one point I was alone again with him, and he apologised for the girlfriend comment. I stuttered that it was okay and he could have said a lot of worse things.

I told the RTVS that it was a 'school night' and I had to go home and he said to wait and that he would walk me home. I walked up to my flatmate and told him that the date was a disaster, but he insisted that the RTVS's body language was *screaming* that he was into me. Then he went back to pashing one of the RTVS's fans.

Finally at 2 am the RTVS agreed to leave. He insisted that I walk with him to his car, which was at his place. I said, 'So I'm walking *you* home?' He said, 'Yeah, then I'll drive you home'.

We went over to his flat (he lived on the same street as me) and he showed me around. It was nice, lots of books. He kissed me, and for a moment it was like a two-dimensional screen coming at me, but of course he was real and I remembered what he looked like naked. We walked down to his car. I was trying to be graceful but my knees had turned to jelly. His car was silver, and we sped the ridiculously short distance up the road to my house.

We went out onto my deck and looked at the ocean. He kissed me again. I guess the date was worth it for the kiss. WOW.

It goes down as a bad date because it turned out that he had a girlfriend. But cheating is such a turn off there was no need to retrace my steps through the seven stages. Chalk up another one on the 'mates' board!

Tonight? I'm sorry, but...there are important world issues that need worrying about.

Movie Madness

A trip to the movies has got to be the ultimate teen date. A bunch of kids sitting in the dark—the possibilities for trouble are endless…once you get your friends and family members out of the picture. Of course adults do date at the movies too…

Age 11 Life was good until our third date. He took me to the movies and when we got in there he just had to go to the bathroom. He was taking forever so I went to see where he was. Oh how I wish I didn't. There he was sitting in the foyer kissing my *best friend*! I was so mad! I really liked him. I went up to him and started yelling at him. I could so not imagine this happening to me. That's when my ex best friend told me that they had been going out for *two months*! We had only been going out for one! Now we have made up but I will never fully recover from my heartbreak.

Age 12 I was with this girl, Mel, who was only 11. We had been going out for a while but she wouldn't even let me kiss her. Finally, I decided to take action and take her to the movies so we could kiss. Unfortunately my friend told her. She brought her parents and it was the worst thing I have ever been a part of. I broke up with her the next day.

Age 12 My boyfriend and I were going on our first date. We were going to the movies and my mum was supposed to bring us! So everything was fine till my mum started asking him all these weird questions. If that wasn't bad enough she had to tell him all these stories about how I got my period at school! I was about to die!

Age 13 One day I kept babbling on about how I so wanted a boyfriend and my friend was getting fed up with it. She organised a double date with her boyfriend's brother. When we got to the movies everything was already pretty bad. The boys arrived late and forgot their money. My friend was broke as usual, so I had to pay for four tickets. More great news—my parents showed up, and of course they were going to see the same movie as us. My date shook my mother's hand. Then he said, 'I'll be right back'. I saved him a seat but he didn't come back.

Age 13 This one time, a group of my friends and I went to a movie with these two really hot guys, Mack and Preston. We got bored during the movie, so my friend took out a lighter and we were just playing around until my other friend's pants caught on fire. It was really bad and we got kicked out of the movies.

Age 15 This guy I didn't really like asked me out, but I didn't want to say no. We were only at the movies for about fifteen minutes and he had already put his arm around me. I was okay with that, so I continued to watch the movie. Then all of a sudden he whispered in my ear 'Can I have a kiss?' Before I could answer, he started to kiss me! He was right on top of me and I couldn't pull myself away from him, and since he wouldn't stop kissing me I couldn't say anything. So finally I decided to scream! Everyone turned and looked and started to laugh! I don't get embarrassed easily, but I think he did—he got up and left the theatre.

Age 27 A friend of mine talked me into going on a double date to the movies with her, her boyfriend, and a friend of his. I don't usually expect guys to open the door for me, but it is nice if they do. My date opened the door at the cinema and walked in—leaving me two steps behind him, with the door slamming in my face. After the movie, I told my friend to take me home. I never wanted to see my date again.

The Scandalous Sixties

Beverley, 56

It was 1963 and I was 16 and had my first serious boyfriend, Frank McPherson. His father was a brain surgeon, something like that—very, very wealthy. They had a huge house on the waterfront and Frank had his own speedboat. I met him playing squash, and his parents completely disapproved of me.

Before we were allowed to go out together, his parents wanted to meet me so I was to go to the drive-in with him, his mum and dad and his little brother.

My mother took me shopping for 'the kind of thing that a private schoolgirl would wear'. Neither of us had any idea what a private schoolgirl would wear. So I had white woollen stockings and a white woollen jumper with a big cowl hanging right down over my bust (which was big for my age) and long tassels all around it. The unfortunate part was that to go with it I had on a pleated green and black tartan skirt (a boxy, heavy one) and I wore my school shoes.

Frank had given me instructions on what words I should say, what words were 'common', and how I should speak to his mum and dad. They came and picked me up at my place in a huge, luxurious car. I was so embarrassed because I lived in a little federation house in a cul-de-sac.

Frank was in the back seat with his little brother, and his mum and dad were in the front. I went to get in the back seat and

Frank whispered, 'No, no!' His mother got out and I sat between his mother and father. The whole time Frank was gesturing to me what was right and what wasn't right.

I pointed out my school as we drove (which, at the time, had the highest rate of pregnancy of any school in the area). It had only just changed from being a middle school to a six-form high school. In my class were the Palaster girls who lived around the corner in a girls' home. They used to carve boys' names into their flesh and pass pubic hair around the class in a matchbox.

Dr McPherson asked me if I liked school and I said, 'I like the kids there!' I turned around and Frank was whispering, 'No. Not *kids*, not *kids*!' And I said, 'Um, girls...I like the girls there'.

The whole way to the drive-in I was forever spinning around to see what I was doing wrong.

We got to the drive-in and we all got out to buy dinner at the kiosk. The whole family went in, and I stood to one side. 'Well what do you want?' they said. I asked Frank what he was having. 'You can *order* whatever you like!' said his mother, 'you don't have to have what other people are having!'

So I ordered this bloody great meal—it was baked chicken, baked potato, a whole big baked dinner—which I had to eat balanced on my lap on a thin plastic tray with a plastic knife and fork. And they had all just ordered hamburgers.

After the movie I was dropped home, and Frank's father said he wasn't to see me anymore.

Tonight? I'm sorry, but...I promised to help a friend fold road maps.

The Sneeze

Susan, 24

When my new boyfriend told me he was going to pick me up for dinner in a limo and take me to see the opera version of *A Midsummer Night's Dream*, I was so excited! I had never been to the opera before and had always wanted to go.

But then I panicked because I couldn't find a dress to match the elegant plans. Luckily, my sister had one that I could borrow. It looked like the dress Marilyn Monroe wore in the famous shot where her dress blows up—a sheer, cream colour, and a bit tighter and sexier than anything I would usually wear, so I covered up the top half with a pashmina and waited for my limo.

But the limo never came. Instead, my boyfriend showed up in his own car, late. The top was down but we had no time to put it up again. My hair was messed up in an instant and I was freezing. We also had no time for dinner and had to rush to the opera house. All he had with him was a piece of chocolate cake that we had to sneak in with us.

As the house lights went down, I made a valiant effort to hold back a sneeze, but that made my dress feel tighter. I could hardly breathe!

Suddenly, another sneeze snuck up on me, and all efforts to contain myself, literally, came undone. I let out a massive 'Aaaatchooo!'. The zip on my dress broke from the pressure and the back was wide open! If that wasn't bad enough, when the lights came up for the interval I realised that I had managed to get chocolate cake all over the front of it.

My less than elegant appearance drew some attention in the foyer as I scoffed a packet of chips with my back against the wall, but I was so hungry I didn't care. I completely ignored my boyfriend and went into the bathroom to try and fix up my dress.

I could blame the whole disaster on my clumsiness, but if my boyfriend hadn't told me we were taking a limo and forced me to skip dinner, I could have sat back and enjoyed my first opera in peace! Despite my anger, the opera story was so romantic that I ended up letting him hold my hand.

[Original story courtesy of ivillage.com/relationships.]

Tonight? I'm sorry, but...I'm trying to be less popular.

The Soul Mate

Kylie, 28

A few years ago I cast this spell and tried to visualise my soul mate. I saw myself on the moon sitting next to this guy with a Paul Newman kind of profile and blonde curly hair. We were both looking at the earth.

From that day on I was looking for him, and anyone who did not fit that description was just a stand-in. There are tons of guys in Australia who look like that but I guess I was also waiting for a connection.

I was living up on the Gold Coast and going pretty hard. One night I took an ecstasy and went to a club. I was all decked out and dancing and watching the showgirls on the stage. I felt this kind of magical power come over me as I danced, like I could change the whole atmosphere of the club just with my thoughts.

I had been flirting with a tall, dark and handsome waiter earlier in the evening and I had made a date to meet him, but suddenly I turned and caught the intense gaze of this guy who was wearing a kind of mountain-man outfit, and stood out a mile. He was wired too, and we just sort of walked up to each other and started laughing. It was like we recognised each other.

I think about two seconds passed before we left the club together. I forgot about the nice guy I made a date with and took this guy home. When he took off his hat I could see that this was him—my soul mate. We had an amazing night—we watched the sunrise and talked about power and magic and past lives. We saw a morning star that was so bright it looked like a fairy winking at us.

It turned out that he was a bank robber who was wanted in five states. I didn't care because he was my soul mate, right? And he was a Cancer like me —he loved the water and food…and he believed in magic! We went swimming and shagged like crazy (he had this perfectly chiselled body from driving cattle) and we had a great time.

But after a while I started to talk to him about his life and asked him what he was contributing to society and why he couldn't work *within* the system to change it etc., etc.…He really resented all that but he still brought all his stuff over to my place because he had just blown into town. He started using my electric toothbrush and drying his socks in my dryer. Then he started appearing at the bus stop as I was getting home from work. Then he started using my next-door neighbour's toothbrush and following *her* around.

I was depressed that my soul mate had turned out to be such a weirdo. I mean he was obviously at least ten lifetimes behind me, he was never going to catch up. Maybe if I was an ant for the next ten lives. What was I going to do now? At least I had the search for the soul mate out of the way—now I could be a bit less stringent on hair colour and curliness. And as for the bank robber—not in this lifetime baby!

Tonight? I'm sorry, but…my bathroom tiles need grouting.

The Transgression

Joshua, 28

I was in my final year at university when I met a lovely blonde first-year exchange student. I think she was Ukrainian, she was sort of wispy and sweet. Anyway we had been flirting for a while, or so I thought, and finally I got up the nerve to ask her out. She said that she wanted to see the movie *Evita*, you know with Madonna—a four-hour epic. I agreed with some trepidation.

We got to the movies and I spent an hour trying to figure out whether I was supposed to hold her hand or what the rules were. She wasn't really giving me any signals as to how I was supposed to behave and finally around an hour into the movie I took her hand in mine. She recoiled in horror as if I had molested her in public; I mean not just like gently removed it but pulled her hand back and shrank to the other side of the seat as if I had committed a dreadful transgression. I didn't really know what to do, because apparently I had offended her in some really, really horrible way.

I spent an hour sulking in silence trying to figure out what to do and she was right over the far side of her seat, obviously very uncomfortable. I kept looking at her and she wouldn't look at me. We were still only two hours into the movie so I finally slipped out of my seat and whispered, 'Enjoy the movie', and walked out. I never saw her again.

Tonight? I'm sorry but...I'm engaged.

The Wooden Swede

Jennifer, 26

I'd been living in Shanghai for a while and my flatmate Amanda and I could not pick up any guys on the expat scene. Foreign men were overly impressed by the Chinese girls, who were proving to be hefty competition, and all I could say in Chinese was, 'No! I don't want one!' so that ruled out the Chinese boys.

One night we went out and decided to tell the expat guys we met that Amanda was an airline hostess and I was a kindergarten teacher (she was a lawyer and I was a journalist). Anyway we had the funniest night ever. Amanda made up some amazing stories about being a flight attendant and I met this incredibly beautiful, tall, blonde Swedish guy called Jorgen.

The next week Jorgen and I met for dinner. I was pretty late because I got lost and my taxi driver took me the long way—the one especially for foreigners. Jorgen thought he had been stood up and so he was pretty happy to see me. He kept asking me why I didn't have a boyfriend, and saying that he could not believe that an attractive white girl like me could be single in Shanghai.

The restaurant was Thai and full of Westerners. We sat cross-legged on cushions at a low table. I asked Jorgen about his career and he told me that he bought furniture parts for Ikea (I laughed—he didn't), and shipped them back to Sweden in bulk. He then went on to tell me of his own entrepreneurial dreams. His idea, he explained with his perfect brow furrowed, was to manufacture and sell the rubber coating that goes around electrical wires at a price so low no-one in the world would be able to compete. I stared with glazed eyes at his beautiful lips moving as they uttered minute details of his business plan.

Finally Jorgen asked me about Australia and about my kindy teaching career. I actually was teaching English part-time at a Chinese kindergarten at the time so it was almost true. Jorgen responded to my stories by telling me just how much he had previously hated children, but that his sister had just given birth. He had a photograph of the baby and he told me how ugly and purple it was and how much being an uncle had changed his life and that maybe he liked children now and maybe he wanted to have them but when was he going to find a wife and when would he find the time to get married when he was working so hard to set himself up?

Our food was long gone by the time Jorgen finished talking. For some reason he seemed to think that he wasn't making himself understood in English. I knew what he was saying; I just didn't know why he was saying it to me on our first date. His blue eyes became more and more pleading, and no matter how much I said that I understood where he was at, and that everything would be fine for him, he was inconsolable.

The last communication I had with poor Jorgen was a long email with a tortured poem by some obscure rock star he admired. I never went to dinner with him again, nor did I ever meet such a physically beautiful man. I hope he finds what he's looking for.

Tonight? I'm sorry, but...my favourite commercial is on TV.

Young Love

Niki, 21

When I was 16 I went out for a while with a 23-year-old guy who lived in the flat above me in my apartment block. I had just broken up with Timo, my first love. We had been going out for two years, and he was the guy who took my virginity.

Anyway, so I started going out with this guy Chris. I was still in love with Timo, but Chris was extremely beautiful and seemed so much more mature than all the boys my age so I thought, 'Well I'm young and he's nice so…'

We had been going out for a while when one night he took me on the most perfect date that I've ever been on. He picked me up in a stretch limousine and took me to an amazing restaurant at Broadbeach for dinner. He held the door for me, pulled out my chair and paid me some very nice compliments. After dinner we took the monorail to the casino and went to see a musical, which was *so* good. He even bought me red roses.

After the show we went back to my house. I had the place to myself but Mum was coming home later. Chris and I slept with each other for the first time. Looking back, it was probably fantastic sex, but I was so used to Timo that I didn't really enjoy it. Afterwards I made Chris leave so Mum wouldn't catch us.

Then I went downstairs and snuck out the back of the high-rise we lived in and went to my girlfriend's place, because she was having a party and Timo was there. And I ended up sleeping with him, my first love, right after I was with Chris.

I felt really guilty about it and I broke up with Chris the next day without telling him why. I regret it now, because he was the most beautiful guy that I had met in my life, he was perfect, but he was older. The truth was he had a huge penis, I mean, I was 16 and it was too big. So I went back to the small one.

I sent him a valentine a couple of years later but I didn't hear from him again.

Tonight? I'm sorry, but...I'm going to count the bristles in my toothbrush.

Oh Boys!

Dating is not easy, but sometimes boys have such a hard time, it's incredible…

Age 16 It was our first date and Jill and I really hit it off. We hit it off so well in fact that we kind of got carried away. We ended up having sex in the car park outside the science building of my school. Since it was our first date, I had no idea how enthusiastic and vocal Jill would turn out to be. Unfortunately, she was so loud that she set off the alarm in the building and we ended up naked in the back seat of my car surrounded by the police. That was our first and last date.

Age 17 It was a blind date, and it was clear from the beginning that we weren't going to hit it off. We went for dinner and then to a house party of the friend who set us up together. Once we got to the party we split up with the understanding I would take her home later. As the evening wound down I went to find my 'date' and take her home. I didn't see her around, but some guy told me she was out the back. I walked to the back of the house and found she was 'entertaining' about six guys with a striptease. I just left assuming someone would be willing to give her a lift home.

Age 18 When I was in high school, I went on a date with a girl named Linda. She was really nice, but we had a communication problem for some reason. Every time I would say something, she'd have to ask me to repeat it at least once before she'd understand what I said. Every single time! And every time she said something, I'd have to ask her to repeat it at least once. Very weird date. Maybe we were just nervous. We kissed for a while, so the date wasn't a total loss.

Age 19 One day I met a girl in one of my sociology classes. Well, we started talking and were getting along pretty well. She invited me to go drinking with her that Friday night. So on Friday we went out and drank, and afterwards she invited me back to her place. Soon we were on her bed making out, and she started to take my pants off. As soon as she got them off, I came all over her face—before she'd even touched me down there. I think I got her right in the eye, because she started screaming and saying she couldn't see. I grabbed my pants, ran out the front door, and haven't talked to her since. It was very embarrassing, not to mention awkward, since I had sociology with her all semester.

Age 23 I had worked with this girl for almost a year, yet I agonised about asking her out on a date. She was completely awesome, but I never thought she would go for a guy like me. So I kind of pretended to be someone else. I called her office one afternoon and said I had just transferred to the home office, had seen her walking around, and was stunned by her beauty. She obviously took my charm to heart, because she played my game back very well. She kept asking me questions about my looks and my interests. Then she actually asked me out on a date. I was so overwhelmed that I said yes, but then I realised the problem I was facing. I couldn't tell her who I was, so I got one of my friends to stand in for me and go on the date. The only problem was, they actually got along quite well and are now seeing each other pretty seriously.

Age 24 I had answered a personal ad and met a very pretty girl at a restaurant about ten kilometres from my home. It was the middle of winter, and very cold outside. After dinner, she suggested we go back to my place, but on the way home the roof of my convertible car ripped and came off. We froze all the way to my place. On the bright side we also made plans to take her home the next day when it warmed up. But then a friend of my flatmate's came over, and it turned out he had gone to high school with my date. They hit it off, and he took her home. I never heard from her again.

[Original story courtesy of dating.about.com.]

Age 30 I had always wanted to go on a blind date just once, so when the opportunity came up, I went for it. One of my old girl-friends was the matchmaker, and the girl was one of her good friends; she thought we would really get along. So we made arrangements via email. We were to meet at a restaurant and then go out to a festival. When I got there, I looked for my date, but soon found myself checking out a hottie at the bar. I went over, bought us each a drink, and struck up a conversation with her. I kept looking for my date, but no-one came in who matched the type. Time passed, and after an hour, I was giving up hope. The girl in front of me looked as if she would do quite well for the evening. So I asked her to have dinner with me, and she accepted. Just as we were getting ready to order, my blind date—who, I might add, was drop-dead gorgeous—walked in and headed over to me. She was appalled, and informed me that she had had a flat tyre on the way there. At that point I felt pretty stupid and tried to apologise, but it only made it worse. In the end, I lost both the girls, who left together.

Age 57 When I was 17 years old a girl from down the street called me late in the evening. She was babysitting and would I care to come over and we could both learn to dance. So I snuck out of the house and went to see her. We got the radio going…and were into some dance steps…when all of a sudden she said, 'It's my dad!' So knowing he hated me and that I wasn't supposed to be there with his daughter I tore out the back door and across the unfamiliar backyard of this house and promptly hung my chin on a lowered clothes line. I was completely lifted off my feet and slammed down hard on my back. Well, I thought her dad had hit me with something and I got up and really started running. I came to a fence and tried to hurdle it—and almost made it too—except one foot didn't quite make it, so I knocked down several sections of the fence and kept on running. The next day she said that just as I had run out the back door, her dad had come in the front and hadn't even seen me. I was relieved to hear that, but I had clothes line burns on my neck for a long time to remind me of a simple date that had gone completely wrong.

[*Original story courtesy of dating.about.com.*]

Weekend Away

Samuel, 38

I was travelling in Europe and headed south from Berlin on a train to a town called Jena to see a girl I last saw in Sydney. She'd invited me to stay with her for the weekend. When I finally get there, to this modernised, former East German town, she runs up to me on the platform and kisses me square with lips and tongue. But it's just the beginning because she whispers 'Great to see you!', but also, 'my boyfriend is in the car'.

'Well, weird', I think until I meet him, and it's obvious something has gone wrong. He gets out and offers a hand in an automaton style and he's bald and at least my age and fit, fit, fit—made of muscle—with cold steely grey eyes hiding a cold steely grey mind. He clocks me pretty quickly…I mean why else would she have invited a nice guy from Australia to her house for the weekend? We go back to her cute apartment and she runs around in a mini-dress tempting me to look at her but I can't because I've already noticed that, for some reason, proto-Nazi has a gun on his hip in a holster, and it's pointed at me.

He speaks in gunfire German, which I can't understand, and have to ask her to translate although she herself says often, 'It isn't interesting anyway', and I cannot, *cannot* think of a good excuse to get out of there.

I have already made the mistake of saying I am there for the weekend so our bruised male egos are competing for two days.

He won't leave her side for one second and even pisses with the door open. He keeps his gun handy at all times and glares at me frequently over his shoulder. Meanwhile, apparently oblivious, she's playing hostess in less and less clothing, and I'm just looking up at the sky…minding my own business.

Basically after two days of being dreadfully, dreadfully polite I stand up one morning and say it's time to go and the two of them hold out automaton handshakes. And I go back to the train station and I never hear of either of them or their town again.

Tonight? I'm sorry, but…I'm observing National Apathy Week.

Black and White

Georgina, 27

Bored after four months of unrequited love, I forced myself out on a Tuesday night. I went to a bar and sat down with two very nice girls. I noticed this tall black guy walk in and I thought, 'Hello!' We made eye contact but he was sitting in the shadows. When the two girls left he came and sat with me.

He was lovely and so beautiful. His name was Ziek; he lived in London, he was a lawyer and the son of some Nigerian government official. Wow, what a great guy, but only 25—too young for me, and leaving in two days. 'Oh well', I thought, 'might be time to break that four month drought'.

The next day Ziek called and we arranged for him to come over. I cleaned the house and got dressed then went downstairs to get some wine and condoms. At last Ziek arrived, an hour and a half late. We went upstairs and drank the wine then decided to go out.

We went to a very funky club in an old French building and had a dance. At 1 am I told Ziek that I wanted to go home but he kept saying that he'd come with me 'after he finished his drink'. Four drinks later he was ready to leave, but he wanted to go back to his place first to pick up his laptop so he could play me some tunes.

By this stage it was 2 or 3 am. It took half an hour to get to his place as he lived out near the airport and he was groping me the whole way. Then I waited for fifteen minutes in the taxi for him to get his laptop.

When he came back I said, 'Look Ziek I really don't feel too good and it's late', and he asked me what was wrong.

To be honest, I had no sexual feelings towards him at all any more. I made excuses—telling him all about my unrequited love affair, and he was really sweet and told me to forget about that guy and made me promise over and over again that I would.

Anyway when we got to my place his laptop didn't even work. But we started to kiss and whatever and I thought, 'Okay he is pretty hot, I have to go through with this now'.

Then he asked me if I'd ever been with a black man before. I said no. I think that just put a *lot* of pressure on the guy. He was sweating away and trying really hard. It was terrible. To me he was just a young English geezer but he seemed to have a complex about the 'black men are the best lovers' thing. He made a lot of noise and said stuff like, 'Ooh baby, oh you are so fine'. I think at one stage he even declared his love for me.

I went and slept in my flatmate's bed (she was away) because he was so ginormously tall that I couldn't fit into the bed with him.

On Thursday morning I got up and made us coffee, apologising for having left him to sleep alone. He was much nicer when sober but he still took two hours to get ready, played the music from his laptop really loudly (even though it sounded like shit), chain-smoked and went to the toilet with the door open. Finally he went home.

Ziek called me that afternoon and said he insisted on seeing me before leaving the next day. I told him I was tired but he said he'd call me when he finished dinner. He called back at 11 pm and asked if he could come over. I said no, it was too late. I couldn't get him off the phone—he was getting all sentimental.

We emailed a few times, and the stories he told about his childhood in Nigeria were fascinating—he'd always had servants and all that which may have explained his immaturity. I hope he got over the black guy pressure thing. I learned two things—a good personality makes a good lover, and colour makes absolutely no physiological difference whatsoever. But he did have beautiful lips!

Tonight? I'm sorry, but...I'm uncomfortable when I'm alone or with others.

Unpalatable Politics

Age 45 I was living in Cairns, not particularly looking for romance, when I met a young woman who seemed very nice. She had the natural thing…didn't wear or need to wear make-up, didn't smoke, and seemed able to speak in complete sentences without saying 'like' every other word—all plusses in my book.

I invited her out to a very nice Thai restaurant. As we sat down, I noticed she seemed a bit uneasy and I asked if she was all right. She told me she didn't feel comfortable around 'foreigners', as she indicated the Thai waitress.

Puzzled, I asked why. She told me that you couldn't trust them. Apparently her family had a Thai house cleaner who once stole some jewellery and she said that all those people were ungrateful and should go back where they belong. Then, she told me that only real Australians should be in Australia.

When I asked (sorry, couldn't avoid the sarcasm) if she meant only people of Aboriginal background, she said something very crude about Aboriginal people.

I told her that I'd been to Thailand, and that I found the average Thai person to be friendly, intelligent and generous. The food came, and she ate it distrustfully, poking at it with her fork. I made a point of eating with my chopsticks. I felt sorry for her…but, not so sorry I ever bothered to call her again.

Age 28 I was living in the States and hadn't had a date in a while and I was having a boring summer, so I decided to ask this girl at work out. She seemed nice, and she was pretty good-looking. She said yes, and we agreed to get dinner and go to a movie.

I was really excited. All week I looked forward to it and didn't mind how annoying my job was. When it was finally Friday, I picked her up and we went to a restaurant I'd been to a few times before. We sat down, and we started talking a bit.

I'm kind of political, so naturally I asked her what her political orientation was. She said she was a Republican voter, which was bad, but I don't mind a little debate now and then. But then she said, 'If it was up to the Democrats, thousands of people would die every day from abortion'. That killed the date. We hardly said another word. Then I just drove her home and said goodnight.

Age 40 This was ten years ago and I was going on about my fourth date with this nice young lady. She was a beautiful, beautiful girl. She went to an all girls school, came from money—a fine family—and seemed very wise and smart.

So I take her to this nice restaurant, and we're having a good time, and everything's going well until Charlie opens his big fat mouth about politics. Well I'm from the States, and it's rude to talk about politics and religion while you're at the dinner table. You can talk about it with the boys at the bar but…

So we're sitting there talking about politics, and I really come to realise how conservative she is. I mean we get around to discussing voting privileges and trends, you know, what does the Latino voter do, how does the black woman vote, what are the differences. We're really having an interesting conversation.

Eventually she says, 'Well I don't understand why black women vote'. And I'm like, 'Well…why? Because they're black women, or because they're women?' She says, 'I don't understand why women are allowed to vote'. I'm like, 'W-w-w-w-w-wait…' She's like, 'Well women in general are just so uninformed'. I'm like, 'Really? I feel awkward here because I think that you should be defending this point, not me'.

She goes on: 'I think that the women who started the suffrage sixty years ago to get the vote just wanted to get the vote so they could be considered part of the system…'

She was so scary. I just pretty much said, 'That's really great. Ooh, look at the time…'

I never called her again after that.

A Familiar Date

Anita, 28

Being very single and constantly occupied with work, my friend Gail decided to set me up with the friend of a guy she had met at her gym. They were going to go out for dinner and thought it would be good to get me out of the house on a double date.

As Gail and I walked up to the table, who did I see but my very gorgeous, funny, and successful cousin Eric sitting next to Gail's date. Our eyes met and he got this shocked look on his face, which probably mirrored my own. I just put my fingers over my lips and winked at him to shut him up.

When Gail introduced us, I said flirtatiously, 'Hi Eric, *so* nice to meet you'. Eric smiled and said, 'Oh the pleasure is all mine Anita'.

We carried on a conversation as though we had never met: 'So do you have plans for the Christmas break Eric?' 'Well I was thinking of spending some time in Byron Bay. My relatives own a farm there.' 'Really? My parents live there! I go every year! Do you do any horse riding?' 'Oh yeah, big time! We'll have to catch up and do some riding together', *wink, wink*.

Gail and her date were shocked at how well we got along; saying numerous times it was almost like we had known each other for years. We started holding hands, and pretending to play footsies under the table. It was kind of ironic, because of course I'd had a secret crush on my big cousin since I was three years old.

105

I got up to go to the bathroom at one stage, and to the shock of Gail and her date, Eric followed me. Once out of sight we pissed ourselves laughing and then went back to the table with his shirt untucked and my hair all messy. We sat down and coughed and carried on the conversation as normal. Gail was staring at me like, 'What the?'

It was not until dessert arrived, and we were 'planning our wedding' that Gail realised we were kidding. She was half mad at me and half embarrassed that out of all the guys in town, the only one she could find for me was my cousin. I'm just sorry to say it's still the best date I have been on in a very long time.

Tonight? I'm sorry but...I have to thaw some karate chops for dinner.

A Standing Engagement
Theodore, 30-something

was in my final year of high school. I was tall, thin and so pale that I made Goths look tanned. The acne didn't help, either. Basically, I was a total geek.

At last I had my one official date in high school with an actual girl. A friend decided to a set me up with a cousin of his called Lena. He made her sound pretty nice, so I got up the guts to call her.

Lena and I had a short chat and made plans to meet at the local Pizza Hut at 7 that Friday night.

I showed up thirty minutes early, and drank five cokes while waiting patiently at a small booth in a dark corner of the restaurant.

Around 7.10 or so, Lena arrived. She stood in the entrance waiting for a waiter to lead her to my table. I had no idea that she was my date, but she caught my attention anyway.

She was short and cute, with long brown hair and blue eyes. She wore a tight top, a short skirt, and had a *very* shapely figure. At some point, I realised that this gorgeous girl was Lena.

Thankfully, the service was slow and the waiter did not rush to seat her. This gave me the opportunity to check her out for at least a minute and a half while trying to compose myself.

Frankly, I took one look at her and realised exactly how far out of my league Lena was. Anyway, always valiant, I rose to the challenge. Literally…and pretty damn quickly, too.

Lena was ushered to the table by the waiter and introduced herself. She stood there for a minute waiting for me to seat her. Yes—to stand up, walk around behind her and pull out her chair and all that, which, given the circumstances, was utterly impossible to do without looking like Quasimodo.

So, she stared me down for a bit and finally seated herself. We made some strained small talk and ordered dinner. All the while I was furiously trying to think of anything I could do to relax myself. Nothing worked. Not mental pictures of my grandmother naked. Not even the thought of shredding Mr Happy using a cheese grater and a large amount of lemon juice.

Just as things seem to be as tense as they could possibly be, those five cokes came into play. I had a new and even more pressing problem: I *really* had to go to the toilet. Immediately.

As my distress mounted, I was starting to squirm. Finally, unable to take it any more, I did the only thing that came to mind. I knocked a coke into my lap and rushed to the bathroom.

I stayed there until I was absolutely *sure* Lena was gone then returned slowly to the table. In the one and only piece of good fortune I had that evening, she had 'mysteriously' vanished.

Before you think the story is over, please remember, this restaurant was in the middle of a mall in a very boring suburb. It was 8 pm on a Friday night. So I had to walk out of there past everyone from my high school, alone and with a coke-stained crotch.

[Original story courtesy of dating.about.com.]

Tonight? I'm sorry but...I have to wash my hair.

All in the Timing

Alice, 25

My romantic evening gone wrong involves my former flatmate Sam. Sam and I had always had a back and forth relationship—friends, more than friends, somewhere in between—we had been through every stage…just never at the same time. We decided to move in together after we finished uni.

Well, about four months after we had moved in together, Sam went away for a weekend to visit a friend. His absence gave me time to think about things and really listen to my heart. Suddenly I just knew, because of how much I missed him, that I loved this guy. It had taken me forever to work it out, because I was definitely not looking for a relationship or wanting to fall in love, but it became very clear to me that weekend that I did love Sam.

I decided that I was going to tell him this when he got back from his trip and that I was going to do it in a romantic way.

Sam did not get home until close to midnight on the Sunday evening and when he came home, every light in the flat was out. Naturally, he went to his room first, thinking I was probably in bed asleep, and there he found two red roses lying on his bed. Beside the roses were instructions to go and look in the refrigerator. There he found another rose and another place to go. This continued on until he had ten roses in his hand. The second to last note instructed him to push play on the CD player where I had a romantic song ready to be played.

The last instruction was for Sam to come to my room and open my door. There he found me, standing in a slip, surrounded by burning candles, and holding two more roses. The moment he looked at me I told him 'I love you'.

Sam said nothing. I could tell right away from his expression that he no longer had the same feelings for me that he once had (he had tried to tell me he loved me about nine months before this and I wouldn't let him say it because I could not say it back to him). He tried to be as polite and sweet as possible when letting me down, but I was crushed.

I had thought that we were *finally* on the same page, but it was only me there this time. Needless to say, our relationship was awkward after that. Nowadays we have chosen to live by ourselves and are trying to work on building a solid friendship…just a friendship this time.

[Original story courtesy of theromantic.com.]

Tonight? I'm sorry but…my palm reader advised against it.

Business and Pleasure

Marina, 30

I was watching some pirated DVDs one afternoon when this guy, Kevin, called and, since I had put him off so many times, I agreed to go have dinner with him.

Kevin was a native of Beijing who had hired me to teach English to the staff of a hotel. It was a nice easy gig and I got paid cash in hand each time.

Kevin was 35, and his face was covered in pock marks but he was a wonderful teacher—he seemed to love it, and he was a very positive guy. I really liked him, but I didn't find him attractive, mainly because he had asked me to speak in an American accent while teaching! I had just ignored that request and gone on with my native Aussie accent.

He took me to this Chinese restaurant. I knew he had feelings for me and he kept staring at my cleavage but I did my best to ignore it.

Kevin ordered us these teeny tiny weeny birds to eat. He asked me all kinds of questions like, 'What is good manners in your culture?' With his mouth full and a miniature drumstick in hand…where did I start? I wanted to say, 'Well nobody spits on the street!' I guess I asked him inappropriate questions too about Taoism, which he said he had practised as a martial art. He told me about Tai Chi practitioners who could heat up a coin on their palm just by charging it with positive energy. I pressed him further about it but he became all cryptic.

Anyway he kept filling my beer glass and teacup and when I said 'enough' he just smiled and kept pouring. I just thought there were too many cultural differences there for it to be possible to communicate.

We went for a walk and he was practically breathing down my neck and then we went into a bookshop and he stood *right* next to me leaning over my shoulder. I felt so uncomfortable but he didn't seem to notice.

I made my excuses and went home. He texted me three times asking me to be his girlfriend. Damn it, I worked with the guy! He started to treat me differently at work, being brusque and critical.

I quit the job soon after and avoided Kevin like the plague, to the point of not returning his textbooks—naughty me.

[Original story courtesy of ivillage.com/relationships.]

Tonight? I'm sorry, but...I'm attending the opening of an envelope.

Bourgeois Bomb

Derrick, 26

I was surprised to hear Naomi's message on the answering machine. It had taken her weeks to return my call. Her tone was apologetic—she had been very busy with uni work and finally had some spare time. I called her back, got her answering machine and left a message.

Tuesday night arrived and I was about to head out but decided to give Naomi another call first—after all she was smart, sophisticated and absolutely gorgeous. I was expecting the answering machine, but was pleasantly surprised when Naomi answered the phone.

'I was just going to call you!' she said. 'I feel like going out tonight and wanted to see if you would join me'. She had to work that evening, but was free later on. I jumped at the chance to have drinks with her.

We met at 10 pm, at the address where she was house-sitting. Naomi let me in and asked me if I would like a cocktail. I was so nervous I was quaking in my boots. 'I need a beer', I stammered.

She offered me one of the lukewarm VBs sitting on the kitchen bench. Needing something colder and stronger, I declined. We got in my car and drove to a bar in the city. Being a Tuesday night, we were practically the only ones in the place. Once that first mouthful of nice cold Coopers beer had hit my stomach and was calming my nerves, I was ready for a conversation.

The first serious question she asked me was: 'So, what are your political beliefs?' Ouch. I took a very large gulp of beer as I mulled over my response. 'The party with the closest views to my own would be the Greens', I replied. She smiled. 'Really? Me too!'

The ice was broken, and the beer was working its magic. I could feel my momentum building. We talked and drank for quite a while. She was bright and inquisitive and we shared an interest in French existentialists.

Unfortunately she was not able to hold her alcohol as well as I was. The bar closed, and she insisted that we find another place to continue our drinking. I was well on my way at this point, but there was no way I could say no to her. We got to another bar just as they were calling last drinks and Naomi ordered Long Island Iced Teas for both of us. We'd just got our drinks and sat down at a table when we were told that we had to finish our drinks and leave.

We skolled our huge drinks, walked out onto the main street and headed back to the car. Naomi was leaning on me and having difficulty walking. We talked some more, and that last drink really started to affect me. I was pretty drunk.

Suddenly, Naomi grabbed my shoulder, turned me towards her, pushed me up against a signpost, and kissed me. It was a really hot kiss with our tongues wrestling. This continued for a while, until she pulled away and said, 'Derrick, I want you to fuck me right here in the street'.

I knew it was the alcohol talking and replied, 'I don't think that is such a good idea'. 'Then I want you to take me home and fuck me.' Okay...I looked around frantically, where was the bloody car?

Fortunately, it was just across the road. I was so stoked about kissing her, so damn horny, that I didn't care that I was smashed. We got in the car and I drove.

I was very careful. I didn't speed, I didn't weave, I thoughtfully used the indicator when necessary, but the cops had been staking my car out all night and they really wanted to book someone. They pulled me over and asked me to take a breathalyser test. When I refused, they arrested me and put me in the police car. I could hear Naomi yelling 'No! No!' as they threw me in the back seat.

I spent the night locked up at the station. When I got home the next morning, I got a call from Naomi. She asked me if I was okay, and apologised for spewing in my car! I suppose she tossed her cookies just after I was hauled away. When I picked my car up it stank to high heaven of vomit. It took a whole month of driving around with the top down before the smell went away.

Naomi and I went out for three months, and then she figured out what a loser I really am.

[*Original story courtesy of geekcheek.com and dating.about.com.*]

Tonight? I'm sorry but...it's my goldfish's birthday.

Braveheart

Alison, 23

A couple of years ago, I met this apparently sane guy while waiting for the train—a nice guy with a cute Scottish accent. To cut a long story short, this guy—let's call him 'Braveheart'—asked me out, and I agreed to meet him at a local pub for drinks and dinner.

I arrived a few minutes earlier than he did and ordered a beer. When Braveheart finally showed up, he was wearing a duffel coat over some cheesy T-shirt—and a *kilt*. The entire pub conversation froze and everyone just gawked at him. I have to say that I was embarrassed, but I thought, 'Hey, what the hell?' He seemed like a nice guy, and maybe he was trying to be funny or something.

We had a few drinks, and before I knew it he was professing that 'Scotland will rise again against the English and defeat them to become its own country'. He even had a specific date for this in mind, but he refused to divulge it to me. Eventually, I had to drag Braveheart out of that particular pub because I was mortified when the other patrons overheard that he was dressed 'in full Scottish tradition', with no underwear beneath his skirt. Needless to say, I turned down his offer to let me confirm this claim for myself.

So, I took him to another bar where nobody I knew ever went. Unfortunately, Braveheart then began to talk about the ingredients of haggis…over *dinner*. I can still hear him smacking his chops, and raving loudly about 'the drrrrrippins' and the finer points of shoving stuffed sheep intestines into your mouth. People at neighbouring tables were so disgusted by him that they actually *moved away from us* just so they wouldn't vomit into their own meals.

I finally told Braveheart that I had to go home, and he insisted on walking me to the train station. He'd been drinking—a lot—and as soon as we left the bar, he pulled a lukewarm beer out of his pocket to chug as we were walking up the street. What charm! He ended up spewing on the street, directly after asking me if I wanted to 'do it' with him in the bushes. I told him I'd rather chew glass, and left him dry-heaving into the gutter.

Braveheart actually called me after this disaster to ask me out again. Thanks to caller ID, I avoided him until he gave up. He did leave some hilarious messages, though, about how he could tell that we were sexually compatible because he could just 'feel it'. No, loser—what you felt was a half bottle of cheap whisky, a disgusting lukewarm beer, and a frigid winter breeze up your skirt!

I saw that genius a year later with some other girl, and he was *still* wearing the same 'lucky' kilt. I just hope she got out of her date faster than I got out of mine.

Tonight? I'm sorry but…I don't date outside my species.

Come Out With Me

Brian, 21

I worked with Jason for about a year and had fantasised about pushing him up against the wall in the backroom of the bedding shop we worked in, pashing his face off, then leaving him there amid the mattresses.

Eventually I quit the job at the bedding store and got an office job. About a year later I got a call from a friend who turned out to be a good friend of Jason's. She asked whether I wanted to go on a date with him. She thought I might have better luck with him than she'd had…

After a few long phone conversations, Jason and I made a date for dinner. He picked me up and we went to a nice restaurant. We made small talk, drank some wine and ate. He drove me home and I couldn't resist the impulse to catch him off guard and fulfil a fantasy. I grabbed the back of his blonde head, looked deeply into his sea green eyes, pashed his socks off, thanked him for a wonderful time and got out of the car.

As I walked up the driveway to the house I noticed that my legs felt funny. They felt sort of rubbery and my stomach had a distinct tingly, jumpy sort of feeling. I called my ex-boyfriend who had dubbed me the Ice Queen in honour of my ability to turn my emotions on and off like a light switch. He managed to diagnose my disease as, 'You're-falling-in-*love!*' I hung up on my chortling ex and called Jason to make another date.

Jason picked me up at the agreed time and we decided to go to dinner and a show at the Opera House, a real treat for two suburbanites like us. After the show we had dinner at a cosy, outdoor-cafe in the Cross, with lava lamps and a genuine 1950s jukebox. I put on some Ella Fitzgerald.

As we ate we talked about our lives. It turned out, the kiss with our mutual friend had been Jason's very first kiss. At the age of 20 Jason was a virgin. I, on the other hand, at the ripe old age of 18, was already jaded and quite experienced.

After a coffee I suggested that we go to the beach for a moonlight walk. What could be more romantic…right?

We drove down to Bondi. Jason parked the car and we took our shoes off and chased each other through the water, eventually collapsing on the sand at the water's edge. Jason's arms wrapped around me as we watched the waves reflecting the moon.

'Jason this last week has been incredible', I said, 'but you still haven't said why you called me. Why are we here?'

'What do you mean?' he said. 'I thought it would be fun.'

I thought Jason had called me because I was the only person he could tell his big secret to. But it turned out that way back when we were working together, Jason had a crush on me…even while I'd been fantasising about him.

I decided that Jason had to be honest and come out if there was to be any future for us at all. He had to say that one simple sentence that he hadn't even said to himself.

'You have to say it, Jason. You have to say why you called, why we kissed, why I'm sitting on the beach holding your hand in the moonlight.' Jason laughed and jumped up. 'We should get back', he said.

I stood up and grabbed his hand, spinning him around to face me. I looked him in the eyes and pulled him into a kiss. He side-stepped and I ended up kissing the sand with my face when I fell.

Instead of being embarrassed, I lost my patience. I followed Jason to the car and slammed the door. 'Let's go home', I said, trying to remain calm.

We drove in silence for almost an hour. As we got closer to my place I grabbed the handbrake and pulled. The car screeched to a halt in the middle of the deserted street. I turned to Jason and screamed at the top of my lungs, 'Just say it Jason! I will not laugh at you, and the world will continue turning!'

I looked and I waited as his eyes welled with tears and he clutched the steering wheel, knuckles whitening. A barely audible whisper escaped his trembling lips, 'I'm gay', he said and waited, waiting for the world to break apart. I shouted at him, 'Yell it out! Scream it! I'm gay!' He looked at me as if I was crazy, turned to face the steering wheel, and yelled out at the sky, 'I'M GAY!'

Jason turned back to me with his face shining. We laughed until we nearly wet our pants and with much hugging and fondling drove home.

Jason and I were together for two years after that night. He eventually ran off with some other guy leaving me $3000 in debt and even more jaded.

[Original story courtesy of geekcheek.com and dating.about.com.]

Tonight? I'm sorry but...my dad said I can't date until I am married.

Makeover Man

Sarah, 32

A very good friend of mine was getting married, so I asked the guy I had been seeing to go with me. I was worried that it was a bit full-on—we had only been dating for about a month and I didn't know him very well—but he seemed fun and really easygoing, so I thought what the hell.

A few days before the wedding, he asked if I was planning to wear make-up to the big event. I said yes, but explained to him that I never wear much make-up. He sounded disappointed, and I thought that the question was strange, but I didn't think too much of it. So, we went to the wedding.

I was really dressed up as it was a formal wedding, and I thought I looked good. I put a cotton suit on with a silk blouse and heels. We had a pretty good time, although he was a little annoying; he kept coming up to me from behind, and tapping my left shoulder with his finger. When I turned to look he would dart around to my right shoulder and say, 'Looking for me?' into my ear. He laughed every time and said, 'Gotcha!' or 'Fell for it again!'

I gave him the benefit of the doubt because he didn't really know anyone and it was a long day.

Here's the hellish part: the next day we went out to lunch together. He said to me 'You know what I'd really like to do today?' and I said 'No, what?' thinking he was about to suggest a romantic boat ride or a film or a walk on the beach. He said 'I'd like to go and get you a make over'. This turned into a two-hour monologue about my appearance.

I will spare you all the horrid details, and share with you only the highlights. These are some direct quotes: 'You don't wear enough make-up, you might like it if you try it', 'You don't wear enough skirts, you should dress more femininely', 'You would probably look great if you started working out, have you thought about losing a few kilos?' 'You know, bike riding would really help firm your bum', and 'Why don't you think about getting a hairstyle?'

All this after the wedding, where I was about as dressed up as I get! To my credit I didn't lose it on him. I just quietly responded with 'Oh, do you think so?' and 'Interesting observation', and 'I'm sorry you feel that way' and then dumped him.

[Original story courtesy of dating.about.com.]

Tonight? I'm sorry but...I only date billionaires.

Butter Chicken

Jemma, 28

I was 20 and I had liked Pete for ages. He and his cute friend used to come into the cafe where I worked as a waitress. He was really funny and spunky and cool. He was a carpenter and he had his own business. One day he came up to me at the gym when I was on the rowing machine, and we went out for a beer at the uni bar afterwards. It turned out that we were the same star sign. Pete got my number and I met him after work for beer and pool a few times. We were getting along great but so far we had never kissed.

One Saturday night I invited him to this party that my mum and all my friends would be at. That day at the beach I lay in the sun for an extra long time to be nice and brown, but when I put on my little black dress that evening I realised I had overdone it and was turning pink.

Pete picked me up in his ute and we went to the party, which was at a pub in Paddington. By the time we had found a park and walked into the pub my legs were bright red and blazing hot. We hadn't had any dinner so we got drunk quickly, but everyone there was already drunk and loud. My mum came and I had to look after her. Luckily Pete didn't need much looking after; he started chatting away with everyone in sight. Mum was quite sober and she left the party after a short time. She said Pete was nice. My friends said he was my perfect man.

It was hot in the pub and my dress was sticking to my burnt back. When Pete suggested that we go and get some Indian I agreed. We both got large servings and crossed the road to sit on the grass. After we ate, Pete pulled out a joint and lit up. I had quite a bit of it. The joint was really strong, and the sunburn/alcohol/pot combo started to hit me. I started to feel queasy. I couldn't move.

'Go away', I mumbled to Pete. He looked around, 'Where?' 'Over there', I pointed to anywhere and started throwing up over my crossed legs. Pete moved away and sat with his back to me. I vomited and vomited as the cars went by. Pete turned around nervously to see if I was finished. Mostly concerned that he would look up my dress I shouted, 'Don't look!' He looked away again and I went on spewing butter chicken all over the grass in the middle of Oxford Street on a busy Saturday night.

Luckily I had a napkin in my handbag. I was so embarrassed, but Pete just laughed and said, 'I'll always remember you as the vomit girl'. I started to feel better so we went off to a bar and had some more beer. At the bar we kissed for the first time.

We went back to my place and wound up in bed together having remarkably energetic sex. It started off great, but then I got on top. I was grinding away when suddenly I heard a snapping sound. It took me a long while to realise it had been Pete's penis! 'Stop, stop!' cried Pete holding up a hand. He was in pain but still quite nice about it. I wondered what on earth I had done, but it couldn't have been permanent because then Pete dozed off.

I tried to go to sleep too, but I was boiling hot and smarting from the sunburn and Pete was sweating and hairy and trying to cuddle me. There was very little room in my bed and we

were restless and still very stoned. I was itching all night and
Pete was snuffling and sniffing and he just would not lie still.
He got up and left at about 5 am, saying that he got up that
early every day.

Pete and I tried to date again and it just never worked out.
Luckily though we are still good mates to this day.

Tonight? I'm sorry but...I think I'm gay.

Bathroom Booboos

Even if you think you've got it all down pat, the calls of nature can sometimes sabotage everything…

Age 16 My boyfriend and I were house-sitting for his parents. We don't have a lot of time alone together, so we decided to take advantage of the situation and have a bubble bath. We were enjoying our bath and each other, when all of a sudden we heard voices in the hall and his mother opened the door! Apparently they had decided to come home a day early. I was horrified, and just sank under the water, letting my boyfriend take her wrath. She was nice enough to let me get dressed and escape without confronting me, but I haven't been able to face her since!

[Original story courtesy of theromantic.com.]

Age 17 Right from the start, my blind date to the school dance was bad. I liked to dance; he liked heavy metal and mostly sat on the sidelines. But wait, it gets worse! Every time I went to the bathroom he would be waiting outside the door, which was nice the first two times. When I finally convinced him to get going, halfway through the dance the cops showed up! Turned out my blind date was violating a restraining order which his ex (who was also there) had filed, by trying to dance too close (ten metres minimum) and had been sending death threats to at least two other women!

Age **23** This sort of nerdy guy kept trying to talk to me while I was studying at the library. I finally agreed to have dinner with him, because I felt sorry for him. I drove over to his house and he made dinner. After we ate, he wanted to take me on a 'tour' of the house. His first stop was the bathroom, where he offered me a scary-looking, used toothbrush, and asked me if I wanted to brush my teeth before we saw the bedroom! I said I had to get home, and ran out of there as fast as I could.

Age **28** My boyfriend and I decided that we would have a nice romantic candle-lit bubble bath together. I filled the bathtub with nice hot water, lots of bubbles, and lit lots of candles and placed them around the room. I placed several of them on the edge of the tub…in retrospect this wasn't the best idea.

As we were getting into the bath together, I leaned across to turn off the tap, and my long hair (which I should have tied back) fell into the flame of one of the candles. I suddenly heard the horrible, quiet, crackling sound of burning human hair. My sweetheart was, luckily, quick enough to reach over and splash the fire out. Needless to say, we were both shaken up a bit by the experience, and it put a bit of a damper on the romance that night.

Age **29** When Alex came to pick me up, he asked if he could use the bathroom. Of course that was fine with me, but when twenty-five minutes passed, I started to wonder…Just then he called my name. I didn't know what to do. He was still in the bathroom! So I opened the door, and saw him—all of him—on the toilet with his pants down to his ankles. He pointed to the empty roll and asked if I had more toilet paper. I passed him some. I felt so bad, thinking he must have been totally mortified, but then he called my name again. This time he wanted to have a conversation while he finished his business! When he *finally* came out, all I could do was show him straight to the door.

[*Original story courtesy of ivillage.com/relationships.*]

Age 30 Back in my student days I went out for dinner with an older guy I really liked. On the way we stopped at a bottle shop for some wine. When we walked into the shop, I looked down at my feet. There, clinging to my sandal was a pair of dirty undies! In a split second I realised what had happened. I must have picked up some extra baggage as I walked out of my door. Like most students, my flat was a pigsty and the floor was my laundry basket…and washing day was tomorrow! Talk about airing your dirty laundry! I ran to the ladies room, disposed of the undies and asked to go straight home.

Age 35 We went out for drinks, and then played a game of pool. He had picked me up at 6 pm, so I thought we were eventually going to have dinner, but that never happened. Three drinks later, on an empty stomach, I decided to call it a night (I was starving!). He drove me home and, just as I was saying goodnight, he asked if he could use my bathroom. 'Yeah, okay', I replied. He went into my bathroom, and the next thing I knew, he was having a shower! I just sat there listening to the shower run, not knowing what to do. Eventually, he came out of my bathroom wrapped in my towel. I told him that it was time for him to go. Fortunately, he was polite and left—fully dressed.

Age 40 I agreed to go out with the manager at my bank. He seemed very sweet and had given me all kinds of free extras on my account. We went out to dinner, and everything was really lovely. Afterwards, we went back to my place and he asked if he could use my bathroom. Of course I said yes. When he came out, he said the words that will forever echo in my memory: 'I hope you don't mind, but I used your toothbrush'. Then he went on to explain that there was something stuck in the back of his gums. At first, I laughed, thinking he was joking, but, no, he wasn't. I was horrified! I never went out with him again, but I still get free cheques. I didn't know it would cost me a toothbrush!

Age 44 I met this guy Grant through a matchmaking thing on the net and he came to visit one night. My daughter and her boyfriend were sitting in the lounge room having a drink with us when Grant left the room in rather a hurry to go to the toilet. All was silent until suddenly we heard this incredibly loud farting noise echoing through the house. Well, we tried desperately to keep straight faces, but then we fell about laughing. We tried to quieten down but we all had tears running down our cheeks. My daughter had to leave the room and each time I looked over at her boyfriend, we both burst out laughing again. The poor guy in the toilet must've been horribly embarrassed to say the least. I don't know if he heard us or not but he went home about an hour or so later and I didn't see him again.

The Texan

Belinda, 28

O nce upon a time I met a Texan stockbroker at a Chanel launch in Shanghai. It was a glamorous evening but after two martinis I wasn't. And there was this lanky gorgeous guy leaning against the wall and scoping me out.

Anyway he was blowing through town and I was extremely hard up so I took him home and shagged him. And we did it again the next night. He was very calm and down to earth. Then he went back home to the States.

We started emailing, and at first I dismissed him as illiterate, but he was such a nice guy that he really grew on me and we became good friends.

When I got home six months later I told my brother that I just didn't find anyone attractive anymore; I couldn't muster enthusiasm for anybody at all. My brother told me that I was in love.

I got on the case and started to romance the Texan, telling him how great Australia was, and that he should visit me. Before too long we were calling each other 'baby' and 'darling' and having phone sex. I started to be bothered, though, by questions like, 'How many guys have you slept with?' 'What size bra do you wear?' and 'Have you slept with your flatmate yet?'

He was forever asking me to send him a picture of myself naked—like I had a million of those lying around! I was also extremely put off by a photo of him with a cap on backwards, holding a mobile phone in his conspicuously expensive and impractical convertible sportscar. Everyone I showed it to said they liked the car and that I shouldn't be so judgmental. I had assumed, since he told me he wasn't doing too well with his business, that he was about as broke as I was.

Finally, a year and a half after we met, he came to visit me for Christmas. A few weeks beforehand I stopped dating altogether and waited anxiously for the big date.

He arrived on a hot summer's day and called me in the afternoon. He had travelled with his cousin Ralph, from New York. I was so nervous I had drunk a beer, smoked a cigarette and even had a joint to calm myself, so I was three sheets to the wind. I took a cab to the house where they were staying. It was a mansion. Shaking, I rang the doorbell. A stranger, Ralph, answered the door (was this a memory test?). I said hi and ran straight past him into the room. The Texan was lying on the couch trying to look nonchalant. I jumped on him and hugged him.

He gave me a drink and introduced me to Ralph. Then two of Ralph's friends came over, a girl and a guy. The girl suggested we go to this really expensive restaurant around the corner. The Texan told me he didn't have any Aussie dollars yet, so could I pay for dinner? I said I had some money, but wouldn't really have enough for dinner until my monthly pay went in at midnight. I wasn't particularly hungry myself. All I wanted to do was lie around getting reacquainted.

We went to the restaurant and it was packed and noisy and the kitchen had already closed, but the girl talked them into making pizza for us.

All through dinner the Texan had his back to me talking to his cousin and his friends, but with his right arm he was grabbing my leg. I was so nervous about the cash and shagging the Texan again that I didn't care. I had one slice of pizza and some water. The Texan fed me and ate off my plate.

When the bill came it was 11.30. I went to the cash machine anyway and no, I didn't have any money yet. I had to go back and tell the Texan. Everyone at the table was rich (well compared with me) and they all looked at me like I was a freak. I told them we would have to wait. At the safe time of ten past midnight I went back up to use the machine. They had turned the Eftpos machine off! I was kicking myself, thinking, 'Why didn't I just go home when they said they were going for dinner?'

Mortified I went back and told them. They asked me what I did for a living and I told them I was an actor. They were all in finance. They said how lovely it was to be an artist. I felt like a total flake. Then Ralph made an elaborate show of pulling out his credit card and paying for the hundred-dollar pizza. The other girl didn't even mention money, nor did she seem to have any expectation of having to pay for herself.

The rest of the night is a blur but we went back to their place and the Texan and I had sex (with no foreplay). In the morning I bought the guys breakfast.

The Texan and I had a really good time for the whole two weeks of their holiday and he said he loved Australia (despite his constant whining about sunburn, and the salt water in his eyes, and a cut on his leg from walking on coral). I was sad to see him go. Ralph I was not sad to say goodbye to—unconcerned for his rep down under he had been the biggest sleaze bucket in the universe, like the holiday was some kind of 'last hurrah'.

But when I spoke to the Texan afterwards he said he couldn't just drop everything and come and live in Australia—he had two houses and a business and, of course, his car to look after. He said he would look into moving down here in a year, but 'I reckon y'all hang out and party too much for me'. Yeah whatever…my passionate emails to him slowly petered out.

Tonight? I'm sorry but…I have to clean my toilet.

133

Double Meaning

Eleanor, 46

Let me share with you my one and only bad date. I had met this man, Henry, through the Internet. We chatted for five months, with occasional phone calls, until he asked me out on a date. We arranged to meet at a fancy-schmancy restaurant with a bar about half an hour away from my house.

I went there on the decided night, around happy hour, and started to look for Henry—tall, brown hair, average build, and brown eyes. But, I had never even seen a picture of him. The bar was packed, and I could see about twenty guys who fitted that description—it was like searching for a needle in a haystack. After hopelessly looking around the restaurant for about fifteen minutes, I decided to see if I could recognise him by his voice.

It was such a classy place, and I was way too embarrassed to even think of asking any of these men if they were Henry, or to tell them I was looking for someone I had met through the Internet. I merely went up to each of the tall, brown-haired men with average build and brown eyes, one by one, and delivered variations of the same line: 'Hello! How are you? Isn't this a nice evening? What brings you here?'

After five seconds of conversation and no success, I'd walk away. But one of these men I approached, who seemed to fit Henry's description, was apparently getting the impression that I was interested in him. After repeating my line and listening to see if his voice matched my Internet man, I turned to walk away. This guy grabbed me by the hand and pulled me to him.

I was *very* confused about what was happening. He seductively whispered, 'I know what you're up to'. I was dumbfounded. Was he insinuating that I was looking for sex? That I was a criminal? That I wanted to bear his children? I don't know! I wrenched my hand from his grasp and stalked out of the joint.

Needless to say, I was wondering afterward what had happened to Henry. Later, I found out he was one of the many men I talked to. Next time (should this ever happen again), I won't be so subtle. I'll stand at the door and shout if I have to, but never again will I go into a bar and approach twenty men in a row!

Tonight? I'm sorry but...I don't want to ruin our friendship.

Getting to Know You

Samantha, 17

I really liked Leon, who I met at school, and all my friends wanted to get us together. Finally we went on a date and I thought it'd be a dream. It was far from it.

First, my parents wouldn't let me go with him alone unless they met him. I didn't want them to meet him, so my friend and her boyfriend came along. Then we were driving to the restaurant, but we made a few wrong turns and got lost.

We finally got to the restaurant two hours late for our booking. We were really dressed up because it was such a fancy place, but then a car sped by and splashed mud all over us. The manager seated us anyway. Then, Leon told a joke, and my friend laughed so hard some chicken flew out of her mouth, hurled across the room and hit some fat old businessman in the eye. Since I was sitting so close he assumed that I had thrown it at him and called the manager.

With some profound apologies and promises, I finally got the manager to leave us alone, but then I stood up to go to the ladies room and tripped over my own feet. Frantically I grabbed for something so that I wouldn't fall, and it was the tablecloth of the fat old businessman. I fell anyway, and the whole tablecloth came with me, sending steak and red wine flying everywhere!

The manager marched over with his eyes bulging out of his head and his face as red as a beetroot. He stood over me where I sat covered in mud and food and hissed, 'Excuse me young lady but I will have to ask you and your friends to leave the premises immediately'.

We all shuffled up to the counter to pay, but then Leon realised he had left his wallet in the car. He went out to the car but it was locked with the keys in it. My friend's date didn't have enough money for all four meals, only their two, so we called my parents who gave the restaurant their credit card number, and then we called the NRMA. By this stage the manager was close to tears, but he let us wait in the foyer.

After the NRMA man opened the car we headed home, stopping to get some petrol. I realised that it was now 10 pm so we called our parents and told them we were going to be late. Then we got a flat tyre. We walked back to the petrol station and called another NRMA man to come out and fix it for us.

On the way home my friend's boyfriend drove. Leon and I were in the back seat and I was leaning on him, falling asleep when we started kissing. My friend turned around and looked at us and we were surprised when we saw her and tried to pull away, but Leon didn't get his tongue back in fast enough and slobbered all over my cheek! She laughed hysterically, almost making her boyfriend get in an accident, so the rest of the way home we sat in silence.

When we got to Leon's house he offered for us to come in to try to clean our clothes. We walked in and his parents were completely nude on the sofa going at it! Leon was so embarrassed and they were shocked because they didn't hear us come in until he screamed, 'Mum! Dad!' They fell off the couch on the floor before going to get dressed.

Leon drove me home, and he told me he didn't think I'd say

yes, but he wanted me to be his girlfriend. I was so happy. We started kissing again, and my little brother came out in his Superman footsie pyjamas with a toy laser gun shouting, 'Attack! Stop eating Samantha!' And he made all these gun noises. I was so embarrassed, but at least my parents weren't doing it right there!

Luckily, we're still going out and it's been a year and three weeks since that date from hell.

Tonight? I'm sorry but...it's that time of the month again.

Go Fish

Chloe, 38

I had a blind date set up by a mutual friend. Simon seemed like a quiet type but he was very good-looking, although not much taller than me (and I'm not so tall…). We went to a movie, which was nice, but not much happened after that. Simon said he was getting up very early the next day to go fishing. He invited me to go with him and, since I love fishing and hadn't been in years, I accepted.

We left very early, arriving at the boat ramp at dawn. Simon put his small speedboat into the water and off we went down the river. We had been fishing for about an hour and I had to go to the loo. I let Simon know about this; he looked irritated but started the engine and headed across the river to a port-a-loo. He pulled up at the ramp, got out and stood there holding onto the boat by a rope.

Now, I was very experienced with boats, but somehow as I was getting out, I ended up with one foot on the ramp and the other one in the boat. Yep, that's right—I fell into the murky brown water with a huge splash. I'm the type who sees the funny side when things go wrong, and I started laughing my head off. Simon, however, was extremely angry.

He swore, reaching down to grab me, and tried to lift me out of the water by my shirt using only one arm. The ramp was at least a metre above my head and I must have weighed a bloody tonne!

Laughing so hard I could barely breathe, I told him to let me go and I'd swim around to the shore. We both thought I was in about ten metres of water. Well, he let me go and I started to tread water, but as I did, my foot hit the bottom.

Deciding discretion was the better part of valour at that moment, I swam to the bank in the shallow water. Doing some extra acting I hauled myself onto the ramp, used the port-a-loo and wandered back down to the boat, assuming we'd just finish our fishing. Simon had a much different idea. He said, angrily, 'We'll just have to go back home now'.

'Why?' I asked, 'I'll dry, it's no drama'. 'No', he snapped, 'you're all wet'.

We took off back up-river. Simon refused my offer to help him get the boat back onto the trailer, but he was having a lot of trouble, which wasn't helping his mood. 'Bloody thing!' he shouted. I finally just walked into the water to straighten the boat out for him. He yelled, 'What are you doing? Get out of the water!' I laughed and said, 'I'm already wet Simon—what's the difference?' Then I pushed the boat straight up onto the trailer.

Needless to say, not a single word was spoken the entire way home—and Simon never invited me fishing again.

Tonight? I'm sorry but...my father's grandmother's aunt's mother died.

Holiday Fun

Melanie, 24

All my friends have told me that I'm a freak magnet, so when I met Adrian, I thought here was my chance to prove them wrong! He was blonde, very good-looking and had the clearest blue eyes I'd ever seen. We went out a few times and I noticed he didn't smile very much, so I thought he was deep, but my friends thought he was a bit intense and creepy.

One Friday Adrian rang me at work, and asked me if I was free over the weekend. He told me to pack my bag because he was taking me on a surprise holiday. Intense and creepy? No way, this guy was perfect!

It was a beautiful place—deserted beaches and high cliffs. But from the minute we got there Adrian seemed a bit different. I found him staring at me when he thought I was asleep. It was then that I noticed he didn't really blink much either!

So one morning he told me that he wanted to take me somewhere special—where he used to go as a kid—and that he hadn't shown anyone this 'secret place' before. We ended up walking for ages along the cliffs, until we were about fifty metres up from the water. Adrian then walked away from me and stood on the edge of the isolated windy cliff. He turned around to me, and with a deadpan expression said, 'Come here, what's the matter? Don't you trust me? Do you think I'm going to throw you off?'

I tried laughing it off and edged towards him, wondering how I could get out of this, while not winding him up. As soon as I got close to him he grabbed my arms and bent me right over the cliff. He pointed to a crevice halfway down the cliff wall and the skeleton of a long dead animal. He told me that it had been there for years and he often came to look at it when he was on his own.

I found that I had to, 'Get back to the city a.s.a.p.'. I said goodbye to Adrian and told him that it had been fun and I'd be sure to give him a call.

However, as a follow-up to this, my family started seeing a lot of Adrian. They kept telling me he was a nice guy and that I had it all wrong. So, at Christmas when I went home, I decided (to get them off my back) to go for *one last drink* with him. He insisted on a country pub, miles from anywhere, and while driving in the dark I noticed something covered on his back seat. I looked, and it was a *Goddamn chainsaw*! (Cue the flashback of me saying 'Goodbye' to my family.) He saw me looking at it and told me we were making a detour to his friend's house to return the chainsaw. So I asked him if he'd been using it to cut the trees back at his dad's house or something, and he said, 'No, it's just a hobby'. What the…?

I didn't get out of the car when he went into the house and I called my parents from the pub for an excuse to get home fast. He dropped me straight home. Strangely enough, I didn't see Adrian again!

[*Original story courtesy of dating.about.com.*]

Tonight? I'm sorry but…I have to take down the Christmas lights.

Laying it on the Table

Luis, 35

I answered a personal ad in the local paper. The woman described herself as an attractive, buxom, blonde professional in her thirties—sounded good to me. She called me back and we met at a restaurant/bar for dinner.

Carol turned out to be 39 years old, 5 foot 4 and enormously fat. When she finally edged herself up onto a precariously small bar stool, her basketball-sized bosoms were displayed prominently on the bar. I wanted to do the human thing and laugh. I did the gentlemanly thing and suggested she looked uncomfortable and we could wait for seating at a table.

She insisted that she was fine, so on we went with the date…She told me that she was a secretary. She was divorced, but only three months ago, and she had four kids. By dessert, Carol had decided I was 'pretty cute', and asked whether I would 'be interested in a long-term relationship starting tonight?'

I was somewhat abashed. Our conversation had hardly revealed the sort of person I am and had in no way disclosed my suitability for a long-term relationship. Nor had I given Carol the slightest impression I'd be interested in seeing her again.

I wanted to be polite. I wanted to be candid. I wanted to say something about the penalties associated with untruthful advertising. I lied. I told her I had arrangements to meet with a number of other ad dates.

Then she got uglier: 'Are you saying I'm not good enough for you?' 'No', I answered. 'I thought you were interested in something long-term.' 'I am.' 'If I wanted this rejection shit I could have stayed married!' Perhaps she should have…

When I went home to bed that night, I had nightmares of a blind date showing up at my place with a guide-dog, a white stick and a family wagon. Scary.

Tonight? I'm sorry but…I have to alphabetise my CDs.

Led Astray

Nicola, 25

hree years ago, my boyfriend started dropping hints that he had some kind of surprise for me. I started straining to think of what he could be doing. But before long he had dropped enough hints for me to believe it was the chocolate labrador puppy I had always wanted.

We also had a surprise for our best friend Mark: I was picking up his girlfriend from the airport to come and meet him. It was going to be a great weekend for both couples. On Friday night, I arrived back with Mark's girlfriend and she told me to go and stand outside my house. She gave me a note. She drove my car away and I read the note. It said, 'With the stars in your eyes and the wind in your hair, don't move a muscle, I'll be right there'.

Suddenly, out stepped my boyfriend from behind a tree. By this time my heart was all aflutter and I was so excited. As we walked in the moonlight, he asked me to reach into his pocket. I pulled out a dog leash! Oh my god—I was right! It was really short, so I joked, 'Are you sure this leash isn't for you?' He laughed and said it was for my present.

Finally, after what seemed like forever, we arrived at Mark's place. Mark said, 'I just fed him, but I put him back in the box, he was whining'. I ran into the room, and saw a big brown box. It had holes in it. I said, 'Why did you put him in a box? That's so cruel!' I reached out and opened the box, expecting to see this little lump of joy, and I found a stuffed animal dog that sang, 'How Much is That Doggie in the Window?'

Heartbroken, but still thinking it might be a joke and the real dog might be back at the house, I picked up the stuffed dog. Underneath it was a box and a card. Well, in the box was a ring. Not an engagement ring, just a ring. I felt so awful about being upset; what girl wouldn't want a ring like that? But inside I was trying so hard not to cry. I love dogs and I would take a dog over anything in the world.

My boyfriend saw I was trying to smile and he asked what was wrong. I just started bawling my eyes out. I felt horrible. He was upset and he explained that he'd had to lead me on so I'd stop asking questions. Eventually I cheered up, but we joked about that day forever, even when I finally bought myself a lab puppy.

[Original story courtesy of theromantic.com.]

Tonight? I'm sorry but...I might see someone who knows me.

Mr Fabulous

Peta, 21

A guy called Tony, who I was continuously running into at the beach and at parties, called me out of the blue and suggested that we go out for a drink. I don't know where he got my number from, but I agreed for my best friend and I to meet up with him and his mates.

They rolled up to the car park in a gorgeous red Lexus. My best friend made a comment on it as the guys got out of the car. Tony said, 'Love my car, love me please!' Right from the start all he talked about was how much money he had, but it turned out that the Lexus was his brother's car, and he was just driving it while he was visiting from Queensland. However, back on the Gold Coast he had a very nice car…whatever.

We went into the pub and Tony bought my friend and I a few cocktails, nice. But after a few more drinks he started suggesting that my friend and I fly to Bali for a week with him and his friends. We, having no money, told him that we couldn't afford a trip like that. He suggested that he'd be happy to fly us to Bali and that we could stay in his suite…with me in his room of course. My best friend, eager to go to Bali, insisted that we go. I, disgusted by this weirdo, refused.

He made numerous other suggestions of things he would like to buy me. Why in the world would he be willing to invest all that money in us? I told my best friend I wasn't 'for sale'.

Although we tried to lose him, Tony insisted on accompanying us to a nearby bar where he spent the rest of the night competing with a mutual guy friend who met up with us, grabbing me and calling me baby and asking our mate how long he had known us. Of course our friend wasn't competing for anything, and Tony was developing into a bigger *loser* every minute. He even tried to start a fight. We were embarrassed and disgusted.

Needless to say we lost Tony as soon as we could. Unfortunately, his brother lived on my street and the *loser* found out where I lived and staged surprise visits in the following week. I told him where to go every time.

A mutual acquaintance asked me later if Tony had tried to 'buy' me. Apparently he does this to everyone, male and female. The truth is that he was all talk and no money.

Tonight? I'm sorry but...I don't like people.

The Triathlete

Carol, 28

I had lived across the road from Russ for months before I realised that he could see straight into my living room. I don't really think about clothing much when I'm at home alone, so I guess he'd seen a lot of me, if you know what I mean. And Russ was a triathlete, so he was pretty easy on the eye (despite having tattooed his sponsor's logo to his left shoulder). It wasn't long before we started doing little peekaboo shows for each other. Then we started nocturnal 'visiting'. But then, oh dear, then we started to date…

So he came to my door in his bike pants and a helmet, and said, 'Mind if we ride Carol?' I laughed, and said, 'Only if you're going to dinky me, Russ!' I mean I do have a bike but I was in heels and a dress! I made Russ get changed and come and meet me at my car.

He insisted that we go to a Thai restaurant and that he knew of a secret parking spot. Turned out it was 500 metres from the restaurant! 'Why didn't we look for a closer park?' I asked as I trotted to keep up with Russ's power walking. 'It's free parking', he said, 'and it's a good way to burn a few extra calories'. Then Russ tried to get me to race him to the restaurant. When I refused, he ran off down the street and reappeared a minute later. 'You're so slow Carol! I've been there and back already!' he said.

We sat at a table. Russ didn't drink—ever—so we had water. I was starving so I ordered a curry immediately. Now I knew Russ was a diehard nutritionist but I didn't know he was obsessed enough to bring it up on a date. After ordering a steamed vegetable dish and denying my request for spring rolls, he launched into the nutritional value and calorie breakdown of my meal. I told him I would enjoy my fatty, meaty, coconut milk curry anyway.

Throughout dinner Russ told me all about the dangers of triathlons and how close his body had come to meltdown during competition. By this stage my lust for his rippling muscles had all but vanished. I bit my lip, politely nodding, and pushed my barely touched curry away.

As we walked back to the car Russ suggested a slow jog, to help me digest my appalling meal. I told him I didn't feel like it, and he promised that he would push me harder 'next time'. As Russ raved on about fat pinch tests I wondered whether he had ever actually enjoyed checking out my less than perfect body, or if he had been thinking of me as a 'fixer-upper' the entire time. I put it to him and he insisted that I was gorgeous. Okay so maybe his rippling muscles weren't so bad after all…

We went to the movies next. Russ waited until we got to our seats and then jumped up to get us a drink from the Candy Bar. He handed me his stopwatch, shouting, 'Okay time me!' as he ran up to get a bottle of water. That was enough for me. When he returned I told him that I'd just received an urgent text message and had to go home.

Poor Russ, he called me the next day and asked me what went wrong and what I thought he should do differently? 'I can't think of anything you could do better', I replied, 'Maybe the right girl just hasn't shown up yet'.

I don't know if Russ believed me or not but I bumped into him a couple of months later with a girl. He was outside the deli holding two bikes when I walked up. 'G'day Carol', he greeted me cheerfully, 'you gotta meet Diane!' I winced, but held fast as a woman emerged from the store with two bottles of water. 'Diane, this is Carol, my neighbour', he introduced me as she stuck one of the bottles into the cage on her bike. 'Nice to meet you', said Diane. Then she nudged Russ, 'I'm going to go round the block while you two chat'. Diane hopped onto the bike and headed for the street before yelling back over her shoulder, 'Hey Russ, time me!'

Just goes to show—even triathletes have a shot at romance.

Tonight? I'm sorry but...it would be a complete waste of make-up.

Same Old Games

Leon, 66

I have never been married; I just like going out with different women and enjoying their company. Since I'm 66 years old, I do not have the chance to go out with many women, but last year I hit a lucky streak.

One morning I ran into a very attractive woman at the supermarket, where she was shopping for her grand-daughter's birthday party. We started up a conversation immediately. Her name was Wanda. She was lovely, and she asked me what I was doing that evening. I replied that I had no plans, so she invited me to the party as her date.

I was so excited that I rushed home and started getting ready for the evening. I shaved and put on some cologne. I even pulled out some new socks. She had told me to dress casually and to meet her at 8 pm at the address she had given me.

I left the house at around 7.15 so I could make sure I would not get lost or arrive late. It was just my luck that as 8 pm approached, I could not find the house.

When I finally stopped at a petrol station to ask for better directions, another man, about my age, approached the counter. He seemed to be going in the same direction.

I found the house all right about ten minutes later and, holding a bunch of flowers, I stepped up to the door. I rang the doorbell and waited, but there was no answer. Suddenly up walked the man from the petrol station, and he also had a bunch of flowers in his hand. It turned out he was there on a date too, with the same lady!

We decided that there must have been some sort of mistake and the only way to find out was to ask the lady about it. We rang the doorbell again, and waited, but there was no answer. As we waited another fellow in his 60s wandered up onto the verandah. We asked him if he had been invited there to have dinner with Wanda. He was. Close behind came a fourth man, also on a date with the mysterious Wanda.

So there I stood at the front door with four other chaps, waiting for our woman friend to open the door. She never did. The other fellows went around the back of the house to see if they could join the party, but I didn't have time for childish games. I left, and have not gone on a date since.

Tonight? I'm sorry but...I can't, I need to take my computer apart and put it back together.

Self-sabotage

Paige, 27

Well I had been in love with this guy forever. Aaron was a Leo—his birthday was the day after my ex-boyfriend's, whose birthday was the day after my dad's. Pattern? Oh yes…

I had emailed him love letters, and chased him high and low—overseas (yep), up rocks, and to parties where I was all but ignored. Four years had passed since we first met and he was still at the top of my list. Now back in Melbourne and suddenly single for the first time since I had known him, Aaron called me out of the blue to invite me to a party. He had asked me out before, but I had learnt to decline, or I would find myself as a third, fourth or even fifth wheel. This time I said yes.

So Aaron came to pick me up—with his sister and his brother-in-law—and took me to this very civilised garden party where we stood around drinking beer. Aaron's sister was great value. We were all having a good time until Aaron accidentally made some rude comment about one of the spoiled kids there.

Then off we went to another party where everyone was very drunk and hanging off balconies. As the party progressed Aaron tried to put his arm around me a few times. This was nothing new. I took him down to sit on the grass and tried to get him to open up, but he would only talk about work, which was rough for him at the time. I supposed he was still getting over his ex as well.

Next stop was my local RSL. I had no money on me but Aaron bought me a drink. I lied and said I wasn't hungry while the others ate. When the band started Aaron took my hand and led me to the dance floor. I was so nervous as he whirled me around. I stepped on his feet three times!

Then Aaron came back to my house so I could get changed for another party. I put some '80s music on. The song, 'I'm Not in Love' started to play, and Aaron sang it to me, pointedly. Then he slapped my flatmate's bum.

Okay, so, next party. We all had a boogie, and by now I was best friends with Aaron's sister. I was still self-conscious though, and when Aaron suddenly took my hand, led me out into the corridor and tried to kiss me I baulked. 'Can we just hold hands?' I said. He swung our hands mockingly. 'Come on, this means a lot to me Aaron.'

I couldn't just jump into it! I was friends with his ex, and another mutual friend of ours was hopelessly in love with him as well. I tried to go home, telling his sister I was running away, but she wouldn't let me.

When we finally called it a night, they dropped me off on my corner. Aaron got out of the car and gave me a hug, moving in to kiss me. Again I wouldn't let him. I didn't believe that he could suddenly like me like that, and I wanted more than a fling.

I called and emailed him and texted him after that night but didn't see him again for months. In retrospect I suppose I could have gone over there...it's too late now. I have to tell myself I made the right move.

Tonight? I'm sorry but...I have to milk my cow.

Call Me John

Carolyn, 32

I worked in Hong Kong for a couple of years and I was bored one afternoon and decided to answer a few personals on a Hong Kong-based expat web site. 'John' replied proudly with the saucy details of how he would perform cunnilingus on me, as well as specific instructions on the exact time I should call. Despite the unappealing way he described his oh so perfect skills, I thought that to alleviate my boredom, I'd give it a go.

Me: Is that your real name?

J: Let's say it is.

Me: What do you do?

J: I'm a banker. Very boring, that's why I resort to meeting ladies alternatively.

Me: Which firm?

J: I'm afraid I can't tell you that.

Pause

J: So do I get to ravage you at least?

Me: Are you standing in the middle of the street asking me this?

J: Yeah, I find it erotic too. So how about tonight?

Me: At your place?

J: No, I'd prefer not to.

Me: Why, are you an axe murderer?

J: Yeah, would you frisk me to make sure?

Me: Are you always this cocky?

J: No comment on that one.

Me: So, where then?

J: A hotel. You name it.

Me: Well, there's the Mandarin, Conrad, Ritz even.

J: Bit of a princess, aren't we?

Me: A girl's gotta be treated right.

J: Let me call you back after I check my schedule for this evening.

Later that day…

Me: I'm in the shower.

J: Even better. Eleven tonight, at the Marriott. Meet in the lobby and call on approach.

Me: You're for real, aren't you?

J: No beating round the bush for me. By the way, are you all shaved?

Me: What? Yes. Do you have any tattoos, birthmarks?

J: No, none that I can think of.

As I entered the lobby of the hotel, 'John' had already called me and thoroughly checked me out from behind the pillar. He complimented me on my boots and led us straight up to the room that he obviously had already arranged. Banker indeed, high stakes for a stock he's never even seen, and definitely not guaranteed a return.

We chatted while sitting very civilised on the couch, or rather me on the couch and him at the desk, trying desperately to move us onto the bed. His sarcasm annoyed me, not in a sexy, infuriating way, just plain, smug George Costanza from *Seinfeld*. I was on edge.

Me: What are you thinking?

J: I'm planning the segueway to undress you.

Me: Segueway? What the fuck does that mean? Who the hell uses segueway?

J: Segueway, meaning procedure. Go home and look it up.

Me: Can you be genuinely funny? Your sarcasm really isn't turning me on.

J: Genuinely funny? That's an oxymoron.

Me: You know, I'm seriously wondering whether I should stay or not.

J: And?

Me: Well, if I walked out right now, I would feel guilty.

J: Uhuh…

Me: But I don't want to stay just because I don't want to feel guilty.

J: I would totally agree.

Me: But on the other hand, I wouldn't mind you just eating me out.

J: Well what are we waiting for then?

I writhed and screamed as he stuck his tongue deep inside me. Neither of us undressed. He kept his glasses on throughout. I kept my boots on. He asked if he could keep my G-string. I said no. I asked if he could do it again. He asked if he could call me next week instead. I said no. I smiled gingerly and kissed him on the cheek.

I walked out, with my underwear in my bag, feeling like a complete whore.

And it felt fucking fantastic.

I turned my phone back on down at the lobby to check for voice mail. He'd already left a message telling me he has a third nipple.

Tonight? I'm sorry but...my mother would never let me hear the end of it.

Single Mum Barbie

Fiona, 29

Before we finalised our plans, I warned the guy who I was set up with that I had a three-year-old son. To my surprise, he not only handled it, but actually offered to take my son out, too. I kept telling him that it's difficult to get to know someone with a toddler by her side, but he *insisted* we all go to McDonald's together, where my son could play and we could talk.

Just an hour after I agreed, the guy was at my door—and he was hot! I mean, a 6 foot 3, Ken-doll, ski-instructor babe! His face fell when he saw me, a black-haired hippie with more than a little meat on my bones. Then, he watched me wrangle my son away from the neighbour's kids, throw him in the bath and give him his asthma treatment. By that point the look of horror on Ken's face made me feel humiliated.

When I finally got my son ready, he started dancing around yelling 'Happy Meal, Happy Meal, yay, Happy Meal!' But I think this was all too much of the single mum experience for Ken, who turned to me and said, 'Look, I can see this is a bad time for you. Why don't I call you later?' He didn't even wait for an answer, just walked away, right past my son who was still chanting his Happy Meal song.

A year later, I ran into Mr Ken Doll at a fancy dress party. He didn't recognise me in my long blonde wig and angel wings, and he came up and started flirting with me! All I can say is that revenge is sweet. When he asked for my phone number, I said, 'I have a four-year-old son, and can see you're the type who wouldn't be able to handle reality like that'. Then, I walked away, hand in hand with my new wonderful boyfriend.

Tonight? I'm sorry but...I'm too busy watching the paint dry.

Saturday Night Fever

Jenn, 32

'd been single for about two years and I'd had marginal success with men on the dating scene. One night, I met this hot guy called Dave at a pick-up bar. He was talking about 'normal' things—not putting lines on me. He was attractive, and seemed to dig me.

Fast forward to our third date…I met Dave at my friend Ron's restaurant. I always trotted my dates past Ron because he has a really good sense about people. Dave arrived fifteen minutes early (which got him a point) and we sat down at a table. The conversation flowed freely, and we were having a great time. I was really starting to think that my three-date string was about to break.

On our way out, I stopped to talk to Ron. 'So, what do you think?' I asked excitedly. 'Closet weirdo, probably a jerk. Too nice on the outside', Ron answered. I didn't take time to disagree, but I remember thinking to myself that Ron didn't know *everything*…

Next we went to a club where my friend's band was playing. I introduced Dave to the band, then five more of my friends rocked up. Dave chatted amiably with everybody. I was thinking, 'Wow! This guy is perfect! He's fitting in wonderfully.'

About twenty minutes later, Dave ran into some friends of his and introduced me—with his arm around my shoulders. We combined the two groups of people and I was convinced that this was going to be a great night. Then, the band started to play...

Three seconds into the first song, Dave became John Travolta. He grabbed my hand and jerked me up from the table where I was sitting, talking to my friend Georgia. I had a full drink in my hand and vodka tonic went all over me, all over the table and right into Georgia's eyes. She screamed so loudly that the band stopped mid-note. Dave was incredibly apologetic. Georgia and I went to the ladies toilets to clean off.

The band was right back into it when we got back to the table. Again, Dave took my hand and led me out onto the dance floor.

The music was pumping around us, and he began to 'dance'. He was throwing his arms around, grinding his hips, his head was back and his eyes were closed. I was starting to worry that he was having some kind of seizure! In the meantime, all of my friends had spilled onto the dance floor to watch this spectacle. Out of desperation I pretended to twist my ankle. I yelped and grabbed onto Dave's arm, faking a limp. We went back to our seats, with me shouting that I'd be fine in a minute; 'I just need to rest...'

The rest of the evening was a bit of a blur. Dave's friends sort of disappeared at some point, but the party boy didn't seem to care; he was busily trying to start a conga line on the dance floor. Yep, Dave was the life of the party, all right. At one point, my friend Georgia looked at me sympathetically and said, 'Well, maybe he's just had too much to drink'. He'd been drinking straight cranberry juice all night.

The band wrapped up the final set and I *really* wanted to go home. I waited for Dave at the table. Finally he showed up, sweaty and reeking. I must have wrinkled my nose or something because he said, 'Oh, sorry! I usually don't have to mention it this early in the relationship, but I don't like deodorant or antiperspirants. I prefer the smell of myself.' I just sort of nodded and mumbled, 'No worries'.

We walked out into the car park and over to my car. I opened my door and got in, trying desperately to think of ways to make a quickie escape. I prayed that he wasn't thinking about kissing me or anything else…the smell of him was literally making my eyes water. Against my better judgement, I unlocked Dave's door and he jumped in.

Once we were in the car, I lit a cigarette and opened the window. As we drove home he reviewed the evening for me, in painstaking detail. Somehow, it was Georgia's own fault that she ended up with a vodka eyewash. And of course he was the smoothest man on the dance floor. The one high point for Dave, as far as I could tell, was that he had really enjoyed his dinner. As we rolled into his driveway he said that he realised how tired I must be, so he'd 'just give me a quick kiss goodnight and call me in the morning'.

I was backing away from him so far that I practically pushed myself through the open window. As he leaned forward, closer and closer, he let out one of the l-o-n-g-e-s-t farts I've ever heard. Suddenly, his BO was a fond, forgotten memory. My car absolutely *stank*! He giggled like a child and said, 'God! I wanna kiss you so bad I just farted! But I told you—that was a really good restaurant, heeheehee.' I was completely shell-shocked at that point. 'Hey! Are you okay?' Dave asked me. 'I'm fine', I lied through my teeth. 'Well, how 'bout that kiss, then?' 'I don't think so', I said, but I *had* to get him out of my car somehow. Did I hold my breath and kiss him or…He just sort of looked at me, then suddenly he grabbed me up into this pseudo-clinch of passion. His tongue actually went up my nose.

'How was that, baby?' Dave asked when I managed to push him away. 'Get the fuck out of my car', I snarled. He asked me to repeat myself, as though I hadn't been clear enough about my intentions. I repeated myself—*four* times. It became a kind of chant.

Finally, he opened the door. 'I'll call you in the morning, okay?' he shouted as I screeched into reverse. The door slammed shut, almost catching him in it, but I did not care—I just wanted to get home. As I drove, I realised I was out of cigarettes and I badly wanted one. I stopped at a petrol station and there, in the fluorescent light, I saw the perfect outline of Dave's body via sweat-stain on the fabric of my car seat

And the next morning? He called and left me a message about doing it all again. I couldn't take the call—I was out spraying air freshener in my car while Ron stood over me chanting, 'I told you! You sure can pick 'em!' Oh joy.

[*Original story courtesy of dating.about.com.*]

Tonight? I'm sorry but...You are extremely unattractive. Sorry, someone had to tell you.

Dining Disasters

The dinner date—a classic scenario, and the sign of a 'real date'. Candlelight, music, gazing into your potential lover's eyes…what could possibly go wrong?

Age 14 It was my first date and it was with my crush. We were on a double date with my friend and her friend and it was all going okay. We went to a nice restaurant and we had all finished and were just about to leave when both the boys ran out and left my best friend and me with the bill! They were supposed to pay for it, so my friend and I didn't have any money. We had to call my parents to pick us up, pay the bill, and take us home.

Age 15 I was out with some friends when we met this guy. He was so, so, so, so, so, hot. I asked him for his number and he gave it to me. The next night we were at a restaurant and he reached over, snatched a piece of hair from my head and started flossing his teeth with it! I was so mortified. I broke up with him the very next day. That taught me *not* to judge by looks!

Age 16 Well this guy Dean asked me out on a date. We went to a restaurant, and at first everything was okay, but then I spilled my chocolate milk all over him. Then I went to the bathroom because I couldn't bear to look at him. When I came back out everyone laughed at me. I thought it was because I had spilled the chocolate milk, but no, Dean told me that I had toilet paper stuck on the back of my pants. I was so embarrassed I started to cry and I ran out of the restaurant. I never heard from Dean again.

Age 16 I went to McDonald's with this cute guy from school. We were sitting there eating on the same seat (how romantic) and telling each other jokes. Well, he told me this joke that made me laugh so hard that I farted. I was so embarrassed but tried to cover up by saying 'stupid shoe'. We continued to eat and I thought I had gotten away with it when all of a sudden he put his hands over his face and started laughing so hard he was crying. When I asked him what was so funny, he said, 'I keep thinking about how funny it was to feel the seat vibrate when you farted'. I was so humiliated; I decided that this was the end of the date.

Age 17 Basically, it was my fault to begin with; I should have taken this girl out to the movies. But when I asked her out, she suggested that we should just hang out and have lunch at school. I thought it was a good idea. We met at my locker and went to sit outside on the grass. But when we sat down to eat, I didn't know what to say—I was completely speechless. It kept going on like that throughout the whole lunch period. I knew that after that experience, I wasn't going to be with her.

Age 18 I was out for dinner with this gorgeous guy. When our main courses came, there was a big, loud fly buzzing around the garnish on his plate. The next thing I knew, my dream date took his fork out of his mouth, smashed the poor fly onto the plate and wiped up the mess with his finger. After that he continued eating as if nothing had happened. He used the fork too! It was so gross. The next time he called me, I squashed him!

Age 19 I went on a date with this guy to a popular Thai restaurant. We had ordered our food and once the waiter had left, my date looked at me and asked, 'Should I shoot up here or do you want me to go to the bathroom?' The horrified look on my face must have tipped him off to the fact that I didn't know he was diabetic. Oops. Still, it was a pretty funny icebreaker.

Age 22 This was a first (and last) date. Wanting to look my best, I used about half a bottle of hairspray in an attempt to hold my hair where I wanted it. We went to a nice Chinese restaurant for dinner and ordered a mixed platter (you know, the ones that are kept warm with a little camping stove). Every time I leaned over my plate to take a bite of food, I thought my hair would catch on fire because of all the hairspray. To solve the problem I decided to blow out the flame. Unfortunately as I leaned down and blew on the small warming flame, it shot about two feet across the table and singed my date's eyebrows and eyelashes completely off. I got a good laugh out of this, but my date failed to see the humour in it. After he took me home, I never heard from him again. Other than that, though, I thought we really hit it off!

Age 24 My blind date started out rocky. First of all, we were supposed to meet somewhere nice for lunch, so I showed up in a black Gucci dress and shoes from Prada. To say that I was disappointed when we ended up at a sandwich bar (his choice) is an understatement. I tried to be a good sport though. So, as we were standing in the line, I started trying to tell him a story, but he just kept interrupting me saying, 'Excuse me?' At first I repeated what I had just said, but after a while it started getting annoying. There wasn't any background noise so it seemed like he just wasn't paying attention. I was so irritated that I finally blurted out, 'What, do you need a hearing aid?' Right then he pulled a hearing aid out of his ear and said sarcastically, 'Yeah, well maybe my battery is running low'. I apologised, then slunk away from the table as only the most mortified girl on the planet could.

Age 25 I met a really cute, nice guy in a bar. He asked me out for a 'very lavish, expensive dinner' and said I should dress my absolute best. I was so excited I went out and spent a small fortune on a new dress and shoes. I needn't have bothered: he took me to Sizzler! He showed up wearing an outfit that looked slept in. When my dinner arrived, the meat was so tough he had to cut it up for me. Then, he *insisted* on feeding it to me. As he did, he made aeroplane noises! The other diners were staring—it was a scene. Needless to say, my appetite diminished quickly. The guy called for at least a year afterwards and couldn't understand why I wouldn't return his calls.

Age 26 I finally went out with this guy that I'd had my eye on *forever*. We were having dinner and I didn't want to smoke at the table. I think that's rude. So I tried to excuse myself to step outside for a cigarette. He said, 'No, no, no! Stay here and smoke. It's okay.' So I did. I moved to the edge of the table and was careful not to blow smoke right into his face. When I finished I discreetly put a mint in my mouth so I wouldn't smell like an ashtray all night. The date was going well, so a bit later I leaned over to plant a little kiss on his cheek and he reared back practically shouting, 'I *hate* smokers'. Gee, I wish he'd said something *before* I lit up.

Age 26 His name was Romeo, but that was the only romantic thing he had. He asked me out, and he wasn't that bad looking so I agreed. He came over to my apartment to pick me up and just as I thought we were going somewhere romantic, he pulled over at a KFC fast food restaurant. I thought, okay, maybe he doesn't have that much money to spend, but it's the thought that counts. Yeah right! He ordered food for himself and that was it, nothing for me. We sat down, and halfway through his meal he asked me to get up and go get some more fries for him. I asked him to take me back home and he did. When we arrived he tried to make out with me and I pushed him away. He got mad and told me to get out of his car and said that I must be a lesbian because no woman could resist him. Tell you what; I'd rather be a lesbian any day than go out with a jerk like that ever again. 'Oh Romeo, Romeo, get out of my face now, Romeo!'

Age 27 I organised a blind date with a guy who sounded hot. Outside the restaurant this weird guy came up to me and said, 'Hi, are you Sharon?' I was furious. This was definitely not how he had described himself. Then I felt like I was being shallow and decided to give him a chance. So we went into the restaurant and were seated. He then proceeded to tell me how he had done many voices for various cartoons. The worst part was that all he did throughout dinner was speak in extremely loud cartoon voices—loud enough for the whole restaurant to stare at us for the entire night.

Age 27 I was on this date with a beautiful girl who I had been eyeing for several months. I had the perfect evening planned; you know, a seafood dinner on the harbour, a fun little water taxi ride then a walk along the beach. Needless to say, I was excited and the date began smoothly. We had our meal and then, after I took care of the bill, we were making our way out of the restaurant when suddenly this police car came screaming up in front of us. They got out and started to pull me aside to arrest me. As you can imagine I was pretty angry because I hadn't done anything illegal for quite some time. My date was so scared she just watched me get put in the car and then walked away before I could say anything. It turned out a waiter in the restaurant thought I looked like some wanted criminal on the loose and called the cops. I tried to call my date up a few times to explain everything, but she just told me to get out of her life before I ruined it…she was beautiful too.

Age 28 I hate blind dates, but I'd been in a dating slump, so I agreed to meet a friend of a friend for lunch. He ended up being gorgeous, intelligent, rich, and seemed very normal. I was instantly a nervous wreck! The waitress sat us over near the windows in the restaurant so we could enjoy the view. It was an unseasonably warm winter day and I'd worn a woollen jumper. Between my nerves and the sun beating in the window, I began to sweat profusely! Things just got worse as the lunch went on, and I was too nervous to take off my jumper because I knew my shirt would be soaked underneath it. I ended up swabbing myself with napkins during the entire lunch. He was trying to be nice but I looked like I'd just run a marathon, and could tell he was completely grossed out. Later, he told my friend that I 'seemed nice' but just 'wasn't his type'.

Age 29 The worst date I ever had was when the guy I was going on a first date with was so nervous (I am guessing) that he wrote cue cards for himself so that he would remember subjects to talk about while we were eating. He kept 'discreetly' looking down at his lap and would ask me a question. This might have been cute except for the fact that he would ask the question and wouldn't wait for me to finish my answer before sneaking a look at the next question and asking me that one. Eventually the dinner was over and we went to leave but he had forgotten to put the cards away and they spilled all over the floor when he got up. I suppose it was a good idea gone wrong.

Age 29 I took this girl out to a Japanese restaurant, the kind where eight people sit around the grill and the chef comes and cooks your meal in front of you. Well the food was excellent, the saki was perfect and the night was going great up until the point when our plates had been cleared and she reached into her bag and pulled out some dental floss. Right then and there she ripped off an arm's length and said, 'Should always floss after each meal'. She then proceeded to floss at the table in front of six strangers and myself! It was our second date and it was also the last one!

Age 30 I recently went on a date with an old school friend who I'd bumped into. We met for dinner at his favourite restaurant. When we arrived, the hostess seated us at a table with a great view of the city. I gathered that they must have met before, because they carried on a conversation for about half an hour. Meanwhile the waitress came and took our orders—but guess who knew the waitress as well? They ended up talking about old times, too. Throughout the entire date, he talked to me for about fifteen minutes. This guy had dated half the female staff at this restaurant! No wonder it was his favourite.

Age 31 It was my dad's birthday and the entire family got together at a local restaurant. I'd invited this guy I had been seeing, and things were going well, I thought, until our meals arrived. My date scoffed down his food in record time; the rest of us were barely halfway through ours. As each of us put our cutlery down, he asked, 'Are you finished with that?' then reached across the table, grabbed the plate, and sat there scoffing the leftovers. He was quite loud about the fact that he wanted every bite of every morsel left on each plate. The worst of it was when the waitress came over to clear the table. She picked up my mum's plate, but my date, with huge gestures, grabbed it away from her and announced, 'This meal is costing a lot of money and I can't stand to see all this food go to waste!' We all just sat there staring at each other. Needless to say, we never went to dinner with him again.

Age 33 A good friend set me up on a blind date. My date was a real estate agent and, after picking me up, he proceeded to take me to all his current listings. I got the grand tour of all these empty homes—complete with a sales pitch. When we eventually made it to dinner, he talked non-stop about how much he earned in commissions. Bored silly with his yammering, I asked him politely to take me home. On the way home, he had the audacity to ask me to rate our date on a scale of one to ten! At first I thought he was trying to be amusing, but he actually meant it. So I gave him a two and (thankfully) never saw him again. He later told our mutual friend that he wouldn't be asking me out again because, get this, I was too quiet. What a hoot—I could not get a word in edgewise the whole evening!

Teeny Tiny Date

Felicia, 12

We were at a dance at school and it was our song. He was leaning in to kiss me and instead he spilled Fanta on my new pants and shirt and shoes. Luckily I had another pair in my locker as back-up clothes so I ran and changed, then I went back to go and kiss. When I was kissing him a girl's phone number fell out of his pocket and he had garlic breath. I picked up the number and I asked him what he was doing with my best friend's phone number and he made a sorry excuse. Then I walked up the hallway and I got tripped by someone accidentally and I landed in bubblegum. It was all over my hands. Gross! And then my boyfriend had my best friend come up to me and say that I was dumped. She also told me she was now going out with him. Then I cried for an hour or so…it was so sad.

Tonight? I'm sorry but…I don't like you.

The Break-up

Jane, 24

I had only broken up with Tomas, my de facto German boyfriend of three years, two weeks before my best friend Sally's wedding. She was marrying a great guy called Ben whom she had been in love with for a year. Tomas and I were invited as a couple.

At the time we were still living together but sleeping in separate rooms. It was an extremely painful situation. I'd had itchy feet for a year, because Tomas had lost interest in me sexually. He was always telling me that he 'loved me like a sister'. Finally I had worked up the courage to end it

For some reason Tomas still wanted to be my date for the wedding, and I thought it was kind of romantic. Sally had asked me to be her bridesmaid so at least Tomas and I could go along separately. I went to Sally's place early to be there with her mum and the other bridesmaids and to help her get all dolled up.

The bridesmaids' dresses were grey sacks (no joke) but we had our hair done beautifully and I did everyone's make-up. I had also lost a fair bit of weight from the break-up. From the wedding photos I can see now that I was looking great even though I felt like the least sexually attractive human being on the planet.

I tried to be there for Sally but I was drinking way too much champagne. When I started to lead the other girls down the aisle all I could see was Tomas looking gorgeous in his tailored black suit. I remembered how madly in love we used to be and how we had wanted to get married. What had happened?

When the ceremony started I went and took my seat next to Tomas in the first pew. He looked at me and said, 'You look very nice Jane'.

The ceremony was perfect, Sally and Ben were just so beautiful together and so openly in love. I snuck a look at Tomas as Ben said his vows. I was weepy and I thought he might be too, but no. The whole church was silent. Sally said her vows, glancing over and smiling at me.

After the ceremony I lost Tomas and was swept away in hours of photography. We made it to the reception centre and there were speeches and toasts. I stood near Tomas but it felt so pointless. He was as removed and passive as ever. He sort of faded into the background for me a bit as I caught up with old friends and relatives of Sally.

Plucking up all the courage left in my heart I walked over and asked Tomas to dance. He said no and told me he was going home. I let him go and he left me, as usual, wishing he was different and that things could be different.

I managed to get him out of the house a few weeks later by signing his immigration papers. Thus began my single life.

Tonight? I'm sorry but...I have to go to the dentist.

The Elusive Elaine

Craig, 25

A few years back I moved from Perth to Sydney. Since I didn't know anybody here before moving, I decided for the first time ever to check out an online dating service. On my third try I met a real sweetheart, we hit it off as if we had known each other our whole lives.

Her name was Elaine and she described herself as a Kylie Minogue look-alike. She lived in Newcastle with her flatmate Kerry who was also single but had a kid.

We talked all night on the phone for three nights, and it started to become a bit sexual. I sent a bunch of flowers to the kindergarten Elaine worked at, and she went crazy with delight.

We agreed to meet in Hyde Park one Saturday. I arrived early, and took a seat near the statue we had agreed to meet at, and waited…and waited…and waited. After an hour, I spotted a Kylie sized girl, and ran up to her. 'Elaine?' 'Yes?' she said. 'Wow', I thought, 'She's even more attractive than I imagined!' 'It's me', I said. She just looked at me, puzzled. 'Aren't you Elaine Waters?' I inquired. 'No, I'm Elaine, but that's not my last name.' Wrong girl. Damn, and she was cute too. So I continued waiting…and waiting…and waiting. Nobody came.

I was so worried that I hadn't heard from her, I called the police and the local hospitals, but no-one had any accident reports involving an Elaine Waters. Late that night Elaine called me to say that she had been in a car accident on the freeway. She hadn't been hurt, but she was an epileptic and it had triggered a seizure.

I sent some more flowers to her home address. Again, she showed an outpouring of gratitude. I insisted that she rest and take care of herself, and that the next time I would come up to see her.

On Saturday of the following week I headed towards the coach depot, stopping to pick up a single rose on the way (cheesy, I know!). Elaine was going to pick me up. We'd go back to her place and talk (cheaper than long distance phone calls!), I'd spend the night on the couch (her flatmate didn't mind), then leave the next day. So, as the bus pulled into the Newcastle depot after the three-hour trip and with my stomach in knots, my eyes darted through the crowd, searching for another Kylie Minogue look-alike.

She wasn't there. So I waited…and waited…and waited. Then I waited some more.

After two hours and some wholly unnatural chicken nuggets, I tried calling her. There was no answer. I showed her address to a cab driver and it turned out it wasn't in Newcastle; it was actually in a tiny little town somewhere between Newcastle and the Hunter Valley. 'Not *too* far', he insisted.

I was going to meet this girl if it was the last thing I did. 'Take me to her', I said intently. And he did, to the tune of $100. Whew. Well, I arrived, luggage in one hand, rose in the other (though it was looking none the better from the trip). The cab driver took off, wishing me luck. I took a deep breath, mustered up all my courage, walked up to the door, and knocked.

Elaine's flatmate Kerry answered. She was a beastly, rotund

woman with more facial hair than a character from *Planet of the Apes*. 'Yes?' she said. 'Um, I'm Craig, is Elaine home?' The ape woman looked confused, 'Craig? No, Elaine's not here. I haven't seen her at all.' 'Hmmm, that's strange. She didn't tell you I was coming?' 'Coming for who?' 'For Elaine…You see we, err, met through, like a blind date, and I was supposed to come up to Newcastle this weekend and stay here with her…and you. She didn't tell you about it?' 'No, I'm very sorry', Kerry said, 'but I have no idea who you are. Elaine didn't mention anything about it.'

There was a baby crying in the background. I looked through the crack in the door—the place was a real dump and only had one bedroom. The flowers were nowhere to be seen. I gulped, 'Err…okay, well, I'm kind of stuck here. I mean, I don't know anyone in town, it's 8 pm, it's dark…and winter, I've got luggage…and I can't get in touch with Elaine.'

The woman just looked at me, and scratched the side of her face. 'Elaine's definitely going to be back soon', I went on, 'wherever she is, because she knows that I'm coming—in fact, she was supposed to meet me at the bus depot but didn't. Do you think I could come in and wait for her?'

Just then a car pulled up. Excellent timing, I thought, 'That must be Elaine!'

A man stepped out alone. Kerry replied, 'No, I'm sorry, as a matter of fact I was just leaving, you caught me just before I was about to go'. 'Oh, um, well, do you think I could stay here? Are you going to be back soon, or could I come with you?' I asked. 'No, I'm sorry, but I don't know you', she replied.

Well that was reasonable enough. Then an idea hit me: 'Do you have Elaine's father's phone number? She said he lives in the area.' 'No', she said, 'but I do have her mother's phone number'. She scrawled it in barely legible handwriting on the back of a phone bill envelope, and handed it to me. 'Oh, thanks anyway', I managed. She grabbed her kid, locked the door, and got in the car with the man (who I guessed was the father of her child).

I walked to the nearest open business (a servo), bought a stale pie, and asked if there was a phone. I dialled the number. A woman answered, but didn't know anyone named Elaine Waters.

By now it was about 9 pm, and there were no cabs in this town. There was also no bus station, the only public transport had stopped running and there was no ATM.

At 11 pm I went back to the house. No Elaine, still nobody home. I decided Elaine must be home *sometime* tonight. I waited on the front porch. I was exhausted and starting to shiver, so when nobody came home after an hour I went around the back, and found the door to the laundry unlocked. I went in. The only furniture in the room was a chair next to the washing machine. I turned on the light, sat in the chair, and hugged myself to keep warm against the freezing country winter night. I fell asleep in that chair, eventually making my way down onto the floor, and using my luggage as a pillow and coat as a blanket.

By 10 am the next day there was still nobody home. No Elaine.

The head on the rose had fallen off. I left it on her doorstep and headed for town, catching several buses and a coach and making it home eight hours later.

Sunday night I continued calling Elaine, but still there was no answer. I was worried. I called her local police station to file a 'missing persons', or at least to check up on her. They went to the house but were unable to find a Elaine. I called the kindergarten. They said there was no Elaine working there. I asked if there was a

Kerry working there. There was. And had she received flowers the week before? Yes she had.

Then it hit me: *Elaine did not exist!!!* Why on earth hadn't I seen it before?

Kerry—for whatever schizophrenic reason—had completely made up Elaine Waters; her history, her looks, her family, her stories, and of course the rubbish about the supposed car accident. All of it was a complete fabrication, including her love for me.

Revenge? Not my style. I wrote Kerry a simple, one paragraph note explaining that (obviously) I wouldn't be contacting her again, that she shouldn't contact me, and that other men are much less forgiving than me and she could get herself and/or her child into serious trouble if she does this again.

So there you have it. And just so this ends well, the epilogue is that yes, I am still naive and trusting and a hopeless romantic, and love women no less than I did before. Shit happens, you can laugh about it, or become old and bitter— and last time I checked, old and bitter is not a fun way to go through life.

[Original story courtesy of dating.about.com.]

Tonight? I'm sorry but...I have to brush my dog's teeth.

182

The Fairy Boy

Rachel, 27

I met Stuart at a local bar one night—he was shortish and had bright blue eyes, a gentle voice and a goatee, he was a sculptor and a friend of a friend. He seemed like a warm, creative and exciting guy. He introduced himself to my mates and wound up in a group photograph of us all taken later that evening. What I really liked about him was that he believed in fairies and magic.

The next weekend he called and said he had tickets to a Mardi Gras dance party at the Opera House, and that his friends would be performing. I was going to wear some green pants and an understated cream top, but my fashion industry friend said, 'It's a dance party, you have to look funky!' Finally she gave the nod to my tartan miniskirt and black boots.

I made it to the schwank new bar on time and found Stuart sipping on a cocktail and wearing a pair of green pants and a cream shirt. I wondered if it was yet another sign that he was my perfect match. I bought myself a glass of champagne.

Eyeing my skirt, Stuart led us to a ledge outside the bar. I hoped I hadn't gone over the top with the outfit. The conversation was a bit stilted, but after we finished our drinks he led me by the hand into the fancy restaurant next door, blocking the paths of the waiters as he stopped to point up at the ceiling and give loud explanations of the sculptures.

Then he led me back out onto the street. He said, 'Are you hungry? I'm not hungry, we can grab some takeaway. You're a low maintenance sort of girl, aren't you?' We wandered around to the Opera House. I told Stuart that actually I was hungry, so we sat down at a restaurant table.

'Let's just have entrees', he suggested, and ordered some crumbed whitebait. I ordered a salad and chips. I offered to pay for the meal but Stuart paid and told me I could buy the drinks once we got inside.

As we walked up to the Opera House, Stuart saw that his friends were performing outside. They were four girls dressed as gangsters, sitting in a white car and miming to rap music. Stuart laughed and whistled and waved at them. They were funny, but half an hour later it was raining and they were doing the same miming and Stuart still wanted to stand there and whistle, so I wandered inside to look at a photographic exhibition.

Finally we went into the party. There were drag queens and dry ice everywhere. I bought us two red, sugary cocktails. They cost fifteen bucks each. The place was half-empty, and Stuart kept introducing me to his friends, and then turning his back on me to talk to them. They were all full-time students, and, as it turned out, so was he. I finished my drink and bought another one.

The acts involved a lot of nurse's outfits, feather boas and plastic babies. It was funny, but it was all the same stuff I'd spent my uni years enjoying, and I was over it. Stuart kept taking my drink from me, sipping it and looking at me with seductive eyes.

When three muscly boys came on stage dressed in wigs and miniskirts that revealed flat, strapped down crotches, Stuart started whistling like crazy. 'Oh', he said, taking my drink and sipping it again, 'they are so hot. That is unbelievable, look at their crotches, that looks so *real*. Wow.'

I told Stuart I was going outside for some air and he accompanied me. We stared across at the Harbour Bridge and started to talk about sailing. Stuart raised his eyes skyward and in a husky voice told me about how much fun he used to have with his ex-girlfriend when they would go sailing. He told me about one night after sailing when they had both got dressed up in heels and miniskirts and painted the town red. Stuart went on to say that he used to get dressed up in drag all the time and that he usually preferred to dress up as Baby Spice. Rolling his eyes at me he added, 'I look hot in drag'.

I was cool with that but I was also cooling off. We went back inside. Stuart ignored me for an hour. I made the effort to follow him around, but when Stuart started sipping the drink of a skinny student friend of his (and then offered me a sip from the same glass), I politely told him I was tired and had to go home. He didn't offer to come with me, so I left alone. We never dated again.

Tonight? I'm sorry but...I can't today, how about this time next year?

The First Rule

Saul, 34

Okay I plead guilty; I like attractive women. It's not that I compare every woman I meet with Julia Roberts or Claudia Schiffer, but like plenty of other men, I do like physical attractiveness.

I was single, 34, and had just moved to another country when this date from hell took place. A friend of mine had been trying to convince me to get into Internet dating. I told this friend that, sorry, I wasn't that desperate, but he insisted. He even found an Internet ad of a woman living in my neighbourhood, who looked nice, and explicitly wanted an 'intelligent man'.

Well, I am intelligent, and I was getting curious.

So we emailed each other for a while and it was fun. She asked me for a photo, I sent one, and asked for a photo too. She responded, ominously, 'I have only one digital picture of myself and I use that picture to scare men off'. She also described herself as 'athletic'. I failed to consider the ambiguity of her words.

At the time I was so incredibly naive that I didn't know the first rule of Internet dating: no photo, no date. So off I went, on my first and last blind date ever.

I went to the agreed meeting place, and took a seat at an indoor table. I started peering around from behind my sunglasses for anyone matching her description. Suddenly I noticed a woman staring right at me from the doorway. My first thoughts were, 'No! Please…this can't be true…*please* ', and then I wondered what I had done wrong in my previous lives.

She came straight for my table. There was no escape. When she described herself as athletic it was an understatement. I know it's not very nice of me, but really, this 24-year-old woman made Arnold Schwarzenegger look feminine. My heart really missed a beat or two.

But okay, shit happens, and I don't like hurting people, so I introduced myself. After all, she had said she was intelligent— and our email chats had been fun.

Turned out that not only was she a bit 'slow on the uptake', but also unable to speak faster than about one word in three seconds, and she had a lot to say. She explained in a monotone that she was famous on the Internet as a virtual S&M mistress. As I ate, she told me all about how she had been interviewed by *Cleo* magazine for an article on cybersex, and had men from all around the country flying in to see her.

Apparently she wasn't satisfied with the attention she got from being 'herself' online, so she had invented seven different personalities that she used in various chat rooms, each with its own kink.

I was finished with my meal and she hadn't even touched her own so I ordered another beer.

And then something happened that could never happen in a movie, because the audience would think, 'Yeah *right!*' The nearby modelling agency (a very famous modelling agency too) piled into the restaurant for a function. Suddenly we were surrounded by some of the most famous supermodels in the world, scantily clad (it was a hot day) and slightly tipsy. One of them cheerfully said to us, 'Hey, are you two on a date? Cool! Having fun? Here, have some wine, we're celebrating our new contract with Armani!'

The contrast was so extreme that eventually I was able to laugh about my date from hell.

[Original story courtesy of internetdatingstories.com.]

Tonight? I'm sorry but...your star sign and my star sign really don't mix.

The Gynaecologist
Minnie, 29

We met at someone's party and I wasn't really that into him but I agreed to go on a date anyway. He had been persistent, and my friend was like, 'Come on he's nice! Why don't you go out with him once? Just once?' So I said all right.

I didn't really make an effort to dress up for the date because it was a one-off, courtesy date. I was playing squash that day, and I told him to come and pick me up. I think he was quite disappointed that I was not in a nice dress. I was just wearing jeans—what did he expect?

He took me to a nice restaurant. He talked the whole time. I knew he was a gynaecologist, but the whole freaking night he was talking about gynaecology and human anatomy and women's organs.

He was talking about himself and his work, as all doctors do, but in his case this meant describing exactly what he had to look at and precisely how it functioned, everything about the female genitalia that you can possibly imagine…I was cringing, he spoke to me as if I didn't know my own body at all. He was using all these medical terms to describe things—his purpose was to educate me—and it *was* an educational evening.

Then he went into his last relationship with this girl, and he spent the next two hours telling me what a horror story she was. And he had this big theory that people who come from divorced families are all weirdos. He was saying, 'I would never, never, ever go out with a girl who was from a divorced family because I think they're all strange'.

He took me home and I said, 'Goodbye…see you in my next life!'

Tonight? I'm sorry but…you're too good for me.

The Mexican Encore

Ellie, 17

I'm very into the performing arts, and there was a major play being produced at my school not so long ago. I auditioned and won the lead role so, you know, yay for me. I had also encouraged my boyfriend Sean to go for one of the supporting roles so we'd be able to perform together, and we were both psyched when he got in too.

Anyway, Sean—who's a wonderful guy—was so proud of me; he made early dinner arrangements at this beautiful Mexican restaurant for opening night. I had a lovely meal, and we went for a walk along the river. Yeah, we were having a great time, and even though I started to feel a little bit sick, I just ignored it.

It got close to 7, so we left to make our 7.30 call at the theatre. In the car, he mentioned his parents would be there, and that they'd reserved front row seats. The pain in my gut started to get worse, but I wasn't about to back out now!

The curtain went up, and I was doing pretty well. I could see all our friends and family in the crowd cheering and clapping for me, and right down the front were Sean's parents, smiling. Finally, the cue arrived for Sean's entrance. As rehearsed, I ran towards him. Unfortunately, I tripped.

Sean caught me around the waist, and a fountain of Mexican restaurant spew went flying through the air, splattering the stage and landing all over the laps of Sean's parents!

In spite of it all, Sean was so nice. While I was bawling in embarrassment, he picked me up, took me backstage to the girls toilets, washed me, and told me he loved me. He even apologised for taking me to get sick at a Mexican restaurant! I did get clapped back onstage in the most humiliating way, with people laughing so hard—but the greatest thing was that Sean was holding my hand the whole time!

I noticed Sean's parents come back and sit down again—they'd had to clean themselves up too. After the show I apologised to them and they assured me that it wasn't that bad and that Sean and I had been 'wonderful'! I had to hug them.

I'm still with Sean and love him dearly—but he and his friends bring this up every chance they get!

Tonight? I'm sorry but...I only have a short time to live and I don't want to waste it.

The New York Boor

Emma, 37

This date was rather bad, almost bad enough to put me off sport dating. Most of the time the men who want to go out with me treat me well—good restaurants, entertainment, whatever. And they are, for the most part, gentlemen. Even if we don't 'click', we part amicably, and my date picks up the tab. This one, well, he thought for some reason that buying me dinner meant a lot more than that...

Peter responds to my ad. He seems okay on the phone; I don't vet him as thoroughly as I should because I am busy at the office with a new client who needs to be entertained. Anyway, Peter leaves, I kid you not, a couple of voice messages a day on my phone, whining about not being able to reach me. I should have called it off at this point, I mean, we're both busy professionals, right? This means we're busy—or we're supposed to be busy—doing deals, making business happen, keeping the clients happy, whatever, during the day. I don't chat with anyone who isn't directly related to doing the deal, not during the day. Much less with some guy I haven't met yet.

But...anyway...Friday comes around and I wander off to meet Peter for drinks at a local hotel lobby. We knock back a couple of cocktails, and he suggests we go on to another lounge he knows for a little aperitif. Fine, except that we end up at the bar at Le Cirque. Take it from me, Le Cirque is not the place to go on a first date. It means the guy is trying entirely too hard. Good cocktails though, fat fluffy pillows to recline against, and nice visuals. I decide not to make a scene and just drink my very nice cocktail.

The dinner hour rolls around, and he asks me where I want to eat. I tell him he can choose (stupid!) and he says, 'What about here?'

Now one thing is for sure, you do *not* walk into Le Cirque and just get seated. So, in view of the fact that they seated us within fifteen minutes of his call, I could only assume that Peter had set the evening up beforehand. Doh! Well, what the heck. Le Cirque is a nice restaurant, even if it does totally peg my pretension meter. So hard to get those things fixed, too.

We get shown to a table that I hate—middle of the room. I have no desire to have people staring at me; I want to look at them. I ask the maître d to move us. This is where the evening starts seriously skewing into the twilight zone.

We are moved, the maître d vanishes. Peter informs me that I have behaved inappropriately by asking for a different table since, as the host, he is in charge. At this point I'm wondering, 'Is this guy at all tuned into the twenty-first century career woman?'

Peter has impeccable taste in wine, as evidenced by the amazing bottle he orders. I would have liked to have had some input into the decision other than 'white or red', but why object too loudly to a $200 bottle of excellent French chardonnay?

We make our way through the meal but when we get to coffee and dessert I commit what is apparently the final faux pas of the evening for Peter: all I want is raspberries and whipped cream. Okay, so Le Cirque is known for its desserts, but so what? I don't feel like it.

Anyway, Peter is sort of frowning at me, and he asks if I want to go on to a club and finish the evening. I don't, really—by then I am tired and mostly want to go home and sleep, but I ask where he has in mind and he says, 'Le Trapeze'. My jaw drops. Le Trapeze is a swing club—yes, as in, swap your partners for weird anonymous sexual encounters.

I say, very quietly, 'I'm sorry, but I think you have the wrong woman. I'm not interested in that'. Mind you, I'm not being judgmental—some people are into that. Just not me. Ever. And *really* never on a first date, I don't care how much you've just dropped on the meal.

This is not, apparently, good enough for Peter, as he then feels free to list all of the occasions on which I have fallen short of his confines for acceptable date behaviour…and that, as the host, he has the right to order everything about the evening to his desire…I stop him mid-babble and say, 'You know, I think we're just not the same kind of people'. And he says, 'So, what are you, a hooker or something?'

Twilight zone theme…I stand up and say, quite loudly, 'You know, I've never deserted a gentleman on a date before, but you are no gentleman and frankly, you deserve to be ditched'. Then I had the maître d escort me out, explaining that my date was a cad, a lout, and a boor.

Ah yes. Dating in the twenty-first century. Whatever.

[*Original story courtesy of internetdatingstories.com.*]

Tonight? I'm sorry but…I have an appointment for my colonic irrigation.

195

The One Night Stand

Bethany, 28

Mark I met on a night when I was determined to get up to mischief. I had taken some ecstasy and was feeling a lot less shy and discerning than I usually am. I noticed Mark's commanding frame from across the bar, and, as fate would have it, I happened to be meeting people who were playing pool at the table next to his. Mark was there with Sam—a guy who I had fancied for years, but Sam was now in a relationship. Determined as I was to play, I started responding to the very unsubtle advances of Mark.

A few hours later I was at my house, and not alone. Things started to get tedious—Mark may have had golden curls, rippling muscles and smouldering eyes, but he was negative, insulting and rude. For one, he refused to kiss me, trying to take my clothes off instead. I stood on a stool and grabbed his face, planting one on his lips. 'The girl can kiss', he said. Then he felt my breasts and said, 'Yep they're real'.

Next, he stated in no uncertain terms that he was 'not boyfriend material'. 'Well I don't want to have a one night stand', I said. As a rule I kicked boys out after a pash or two. 'It doesn't have to be a one night stand', he assured me, and I was so out of it, that I chose to believe him. Anyway, I figured he was just another dumb, gorgeous guy, so who cares?

So we went at it frantically, but then he held me all night

long. We had some pretty funny chats and played around again in the morning.

I made him lemon tea just as he had instructed but he didn't drink it. He got my number and smiled and waved as he left. I was now much more sober and feeling confused by the illusions of intimacy that happen during sex on drugs.

But later that day, when my high had completely worn off, I was deeply regretting having slept with such a mean guy, my girlfriend—(who had been at the bar with us the night before) came over and in front of a room full of guests shouted, 'Did you sleep with Mark James? Oh my *God*!' Well as it turned out not only did a few of the people in the room know him well, he was on some TV show and had previously dated a thousand women within a very small radius, including a blonde super-model. There went the anonymous shag with a dumb, gorgeous guy! My spirits plummeted further into the abyss.

The next night I saw him at a bar I always go to. I had never seen him there before and I was taken aback. I pretended not to see him at all, but obsessed over him darkly for the next few weeks.

Another month or so passed and I saw Mark at a party. I had succeeded in forgetting about him and was not expecting it. I tried to pour myself a drink and found my hands were shaking. He blew me a kiss and I smiled, but couldn't hold his gaze. I was more surprised by my physical reaction to seeing him again than by the fact that he was there. I couldn't drink, I couldn't dance, I couldn't talk to him, I couldn't talk to anybody else.

When he finally came up to me and apologised for not calling I was sarcastic and dismissive. We ended up having a loud argu-ment on the dance floor, which culminated with him shouting (loud enough for a guy I really did fancy to hear), 'What do you want me to say? I had a good time with you!' I went home to nurse my wounded pride and cried, so furious with myself for having been unable to control myself on drugs, and unable to retrieve the part of myself I had given to Mark. I ended up taking the only possible route—I made friends with Mark and played hard to get with the guy I really wanted. It worked.

Tonight? I'm sorry but...I'm not in the mood for fun.

Barrel Boy

Phoebe, 56

I had recently split up with my third husband and wanted to make a fresh start. I had a look on a dating web site at the people around my age and Gary was the first person that I emailed. He emailed straight back. I didn't really know the procedure so I gave him my phone number.

He had a couple of degrees, was in a senior executive job, well travelled and sophisticated, so he seemed fine. After not too long he started ringing me up two or three times a day, waking me up in the morning with 'Hello darling'. I'd say, 'Who is this?' And he'd make me guess.

He'd say something ridiculous like, 'How many men wake you up in the morning saying "Good morning darling?"' I kept my cool and replied, 'Lots. Who is this please?'

He rang me ten times after that saying, 'Hi, guess who this is?' And I'd say 'It must be Gary. You are the only one tiresome enough to do this guessing game thing.'

By then a few other men were ringing. But he still seemed quite funny so I agreed to meet him for lunch seeing as he was the first person I'd made contact with.

He rang me three times that day to make sure I hadn't forgotten. I got there early because I wanted to do some work, and he walked in. He was big—not fat, but a big barrel-chested man. He sat down and said, 'You're a slip of a thing aren't you? Nice eyes, nice breasts, what's your bum like?'

After I'd recovered from the shock of his comments and we'd been talking for a while he announced, 'I have some flaws'. I said, 'Oh really what are they?' I thought he was going to talk about being too emotional. But he said, 'I have three hernias— an umbilical one, a testicular one…' and I didn't hear what the third one was.

He also had a shaved, bald head. He said, 'I have a lot of hair on my body but not much on my head'. I couldn't stop myself from pointing out that he had none on his head.

Then he asked me if I had any physical flaws and I said, 'No, Who cares anyway?'

And then I sat there for ages trying to think of one, and the worst thing that I could come up with was the three earring holes in each ear left over from the eighties. So I stuck out my foot and said, 'I fell over', and showed him my scabby foot.

He said, 'Pretty feet, so I suppose you're pretty perfect'. I started to feel nauseous. I said, 'No it's just that I can't think of anything at the moment'.

So then he asked me what I liked best about myself. I told him that I was really bored with these questions, but he persisted, and I told him that I liked my skin because if I didn't have it my organs would fall out! And without missing a beat he said, 'Yes my skin is my best feature too', and lifted up his arms and rolled them back and forth while we stared at them. 'It's in very good nick'.

While we ate he talked about his passion for shooting ducks and how, for some reason I couldn't quite work out, he hated violent movies because of that. He also talked about his ex-wife and said how much fun he was having being single. Apparently he'd dated a lot of psychologists. The restaurant was so noisy that I couldn't even hear much of what he was saying. I ate everything that was on my plate and just nodded every now and then and he seemed perfectly happy. He also gave me a hunk of his chicken. I offered to pay but he did.

When we got outside we did this really clumsy hug in the middle of the lunchtime crowd, so he grabbed me, putting his hand on my bum and said, 'You're a good sort'. And I told him to get his hand off my bottom.

Then he looked at me from all angles like I was a horse or something and said, 'I like you better out on the street; in the restaurant you looked all washed out. Do you want to go to the pictures?' I said maybe in a couple of weeks. He smacked me on the bum again as I left.

And the worst thing was that another guy called me while we were having lunch, this one was a well-known painter. When I tried to call him back I got the number wrong and called up Barrel Boy instead, so I had to pretend I was calling to thank him for lunch.

So what do I think of dating again? If I thought for one second that I might find Mr Right on one of these dates then I would go crazy. I just go looking for friends and sit there and try to think of them as a woman.

Tonight? I'm sorry but...I have to do my nails.

Three Strikes

Irene, 40

I met Ray on the Internet. We chatted for a couple of weeks, then decided to meet at a local restaurant. The day we chose was a busy one for me at work, so I grabbed some quick Chinese noodles for lunch in between assignments. By the time I showed up for the date that evening, my stomach was churning.

I thought I was just nervous about meeting someone new. No such luck! In fact, I had to make a dash for the toilets before our entree had arrived. I was violently ill because of food poisoning from my lunchtime stir-fry. Just in case I was too sick to drive, I let Ray follow me home in his car. On the good side, I was laughing hysterically and he was a good sport, but then again, I was sick for two days.

When I had finally recuperated, I agreed to meet Ray again (I didn't want him to think I made up the story to ditch him). This time we were going to my favourite local bar. We had just finished our first drink and were chatting comfortably when a bartender lifted a stool above his head—and sheared off a couple of ceiling fan blades, both of which whacked me in the head. Fortunately, no stitches were necessary. Again, I was laughing hysterically, because I couldn't believe that this was happening to me.

After driving home and putting ice on my head, I decided to give it one more try. Ray was such a nice guy, and there aren't many around! So, we decided to meet for coffee. But after the waiter spilled a scalding cappuccino on my lap, I decided that Ray should just send me a postcard, preferably from far, far away. Nice guy or not, at this rate, I reckoned that with that kind of karma happening I'd eventually end up needing hospitalisation!

[Original story courtesy of ivillage.com/relationships.]

Tonight? I'm sorry but...I just couldn't be bothered.

Tragic Distractions

Millie, 30

A friend of mine wanted to set me up with Todd, a mate of her husband's brother. I spoke to him over the phone a few times and he seemed really lovely—he was funny, smart and a successful designer. We were supposed to be properly introduced at my twenty-ninth birthday party, where there would be lots of people and no pressure.

On the day before my birthday, Todd rang to say he couldn't come to my party the next night because he had to fly to Melbourne in the morning on an 'urgent family matter'. He apologised profusely and asked me to have dinner with him that night. I agreed because I wasn't doing anything anyway.

We met at a tapas bar and I was pretty pleased with his looks, but I thought he must have been disappointed in me or just very nervous, because he seemed a lot more serious than when I'd spoken to him on the phone. The whole evening he was nice but somehow distracted, and only moved his food around with his fork. I felt badly because I had suggested this restaurant, and he clearly wasn't into it.

I tried to be interesting and engage him, thinking that if he didn't like me in *that* way we could probably be friends. I said, 'Beck mentioned that your dad is a barrister, is that right?' Todd replied, 'My father *was* a barrister…' 'Great way to lighten the mood Millie!' I thought, wishing I had kept my mouth shut. I

offered my sympathies, said I'd had no idea, and asked him when his father had died.

Todd took a breath: 'Well, actually, he committed suicide over the weekend, we think. My brother went over to Dad's place this morning and found him hanging from a beam in the garage. I have to go to Melbourne for the funeral and stuff so that's why I have to miss your party.'

I swear to *God* that this really happened. My jaw dropped of course, and Todd said feebly, 'It's okay, it's okay'. Then he just sat there staring at the floor with this glazed look on his face. I suggested that we leave—he nodded vaguely—and quickly paid the bill.

The end of the story is that I drove Todd home, packed a suit-case for him with a dark suit and other essentials, let him sleep on my couch, drove him to the airport in the morning, took his wallet out of his pants to buy him a plane ticket, put him on the plane and then called my friends to tell them what had happened. He was obviously in shock so I did what I had to do.

Needless to say, the budding romance never quite took off, but Todd and I remain friends to this day.

Tonight? I'm sorry but...I have to follow my heart.

Wet Nightmare

Bill, 50-something

This is a horror story I have never told anyone before. You won't ask why not! I had just separated from my wife and moved in with a new girlfriend. My girlfriend had lent me her car to get to a job three hours out of town—I could have it for two weeks, and then she would take it for one week. She was a really nice girl.

After a week of working on this job, I started to flirt with the waitress in the cafe where the crew ate. I asked her out on a date, and she accepted. I picked her up at her place, and after talking for a bit, we began to neck.

We were doing a lot of kissing, and getting very hot, and then she asked me to take her to bed to make love to her. When we got naked, the trouble started. I couldn't get it up. For the first time in my life I just could not get an erection. Maybe it was guilt. Nothing I did made any difference. Eventually, I had to roll over and we went to sleep.

I felt terrible. I was embarrassed, but worse than that, I knew I was cheating on a very sweet girl. In the middle of the night, I woke from a terrible nightmare. The sheets were all wet, but it wasn't sweat and it wasn't lovemaking—I had wet her bed! I hadn't done that since I was 14 (I was a bed wetter until then). At the time, I was 28.

I lay awake all night to make sure that she didn't roll over into the huge wet patch, and I left in the morning without mentioning my accident. She didn't say anything, so I assume she hadn't noticed…yet. I avoided her by not going back to the restaurant, and of course, she made no attempt to call me either. This was twenty-five years ago.

I am revolted by my behaviour whenever I think about that incident, but to my credit, I never did anything like it again. I eventually went back to my wife and I never told a soul.

[Original story courtesy of dating.about.com.]

Tonight? I'm sorry but…no.

The Date Who Made Me Cross

Lesley, 22

New in town and happy for an opportunity to 'see some of the sights' as promised by Graeme, I accepted a Thursday night date. We would be going to a place in town that didn't serve alcohol and had stage shows which were 'very entertaining' he assured me. It sounded safe, interesting, and I was really looking forward to seeing the city. Graeme was sweet, funny, tall, dark and handsome. How could I lose?

When he arrived to pick me up, Graeme told me that I was overdressed in my skirt and blouse. I agreed to change into jeans and a man's shirt that he'd brought along 'just in case I didn't have one'. He then convinced me to remove my make-up and pull my hair back into a ponytail, and off we went.

When we arrived at the restaurant I could see that there were many different people there of all kinds and all ages, and there was a buzz of excitement in the air. There was indeed a stage, and candlelit tables. We took a seat. But, just as the lights started to dim, Graeme excused himself from the table. The first musical cord struck, the spotlight splashed on the sparkled curtain, and a woman who looked like Liza Minnelli stepped out from behind it. She belted out, 'Life is a cabaret!' and rocked the house.

As 'Liza' bowed to the cheering audience I looked around for Graeme, who still hadn't returned. I thought I heard his voice in the crowd so I got up and walked around—no sign of him. I went to the bathroom. In every stall, except the empty one I went into, there were two sets of feet.

Suddenly there was a knock at my toilet door. I said, 'Someone is in here.' They said, 'I know, you don't want company?' and giggled. After washing up rather hastily, I ran back to our table. Still no Graeme. I was starting to get very nervous. Out walks 'Diana Ross' and I hear Graeme giggling and saying something about having to get back to his table. He was somewhere close by…

My eyes pierced the darkness of the room. I focused on where the sound of Graeme's giggles were coming from…I stood up and I heard him again. I walked towards a couple— a woman in a white dress sitting on a man's lap—and again the giggle. Then I saw him, the woman in the white dress was Graeme! He had a beautiful low-cut, sequined satin gown on and was wearing white satin heels. He was whispering coquettishly into the gentleman's ear. When he saw me staring at them, he waved a gloved hand.

I ran from the place, pushing through the crowd, gasping for air. I hailed a cab that was parked just outside and got in. As we drove away, I looked back to see Graeme holding up his gown and waving frantically to the cabbie to stop. He was calling out to me to come back, yelling, 'Lesley, *dahling*! What's wrong?'

Tonight? I'm sorry but…It's my parakeet's bowling night.

The Big Sleep

Rhiannon, 28

I met this guy at a party on the beach. He wearing a very cute hat and a very silly T-shirt. He was hot really, I don't know what it was, but there was something about him. He was tall, dark, handsome and strangely magnetic. All my girlfriends crowded around him but he ended up going home with me because I fought them off, I wanted him. Bad.

He was really funny and really nice. Unfortunately I had just read *The Rules* so I decided I couldn't sleep with him. We kissed on the couch and it was so sexy I was absolutely on fire. I made him take my number and told him that we had to date before we did anything. I don't know if he was used to that kind of treatment.

Eventually he did call and we made a date. But the day of the date came and I was totally sick with the flu. I took some cold and flu tablets, but instead of taking the daytime ones that wake you up, I accidentally took the nighttime ones.

All he had asked was that I bring some food, because we were going on a picnic. I made guacamole and got some salsa and Turkish bread, but I thought we could buy a chicken or something.

He was late, and I made a comment about him being as disorganised as I was but he didn't think that was funny. I was so nervous. We picked up some wine (but no chicken) and went to the movies in the park.

We lay down under a tree on the rug. I kept having to go to the toilet. The movie was in Spanish, and very arty. It was about teenage boys and how horny they are. He was really hungry but he didn't eat my dip, maybe there was too much garlic in it. He bought a pie and ate that instead.

He kept asking me if this was the perfect first date. I said yes, and I was having fun, but I was so sleepy. I lay my head down on his shoulder. He was so cuddly that I fell asleep.

When the movie was over I woke up. My date was obviously not impressed in the slightest. He drove me home and we went upstairs. There, to make matters worse, we discovered my crazy flatmate and her crazy boyfriend, smoking marijuana and playing scrabble. They wanted to have a bright and energetic conversation.

As soon as we could we went into the bedroom. I let him get to second base and then I chased him off home because I was sick.

I saw him a few weeks later with another girl.

A year went by and we kept seeing each other out all the time. Every time there was chemistry and sometimes we snuck off to pash. We had to sneak because his best friend had started liking me. Once I even took him home but *again* we couldn't do it because I had my period.

Last weekend I finally I admitted to myself that I liked this guy and he admitted that he still liked me even though I was a terrible date. We agreed to go out again. He made me promise that this time I would sleep with him. I promised. That date is tonight and guess what…I have come out in a terrible, itchy rash.

Tonight? I'm sorry but…I prefer not to masticate in public.

The Secret Video

Harry, 30

I met this guy online; we did the photo thing and the video conferencing thing deep into the night. He was totally hot. One night we went out for a boogie. He walked in looking like a complete babe, wearing a tight little singlet. He was totally cut—six-pack and everything. He walked straight over to me and kissed me. The chemistry was amazing; I was ready to go home with him right then, but we stayed at the bar and got pretty hammered.

He was an awesome dancer too and we were going for it, then we starting kissing and we were all over each other on the dance floor. Suddenly my best friend, who I'd had no idea was there at the club, came up to us. I told him to go away and that I would give him all the juicy details the next day.

So anyway, my date and I went back to his house and we shagged all night long. I remember noticing that his computer was turned on but I didn't think anything of it at the time. It was the best night of my life. I was totally in love.

The next morning I went home and crashed out. I was woken up at about four in the arvo by my best mate. He goes, 'Well good morning Mr Dynamo, didn't you have a lot of fun last night!' I said, 'Yeah sorry for ditching you in the club, I was on a hot date'. And he said, 'I know all about it. He's a very talented boy and so are you! I had no idea Harry.' I was like, 'We were just kissing…sorry but I got a bit carried away'. 'You sure did', he said, 'I was watching you for five hours!'

I started to go cold all over. It turned out that my all night sex romp had been broadcast live to the cyber world from this guy's bedroom. I was a porn star.

Luckily nobody ever recognised me from the Internet, but I couldn't look my best friend in the eye for a loooong time, I mean he watched it for *five hours!* I know I'm good in bed but uninvited visitors don't do it for me. I never called video porn boy ever again.

Tonight? I'm sorry but…I just couldn't face another disastrous date.

55 Ways To Shake Off a Sticky Date

If all else fails and a date is going so badly that you have to get out of there, here are some surefire ways to turn your date off!

1. At dinner, guard your plate with a steak knife, so as to give the impression that you'll stab anyone, including the waiter, who reaches for it.

2. Collect the salt shakers from all of the tables in the restaurant, and balance them in a tower on your table.

3. Wipe your nose on your date's sleeve. Twice.

4. Make funny faces at other patrons, and then sneer at their reactions.

5. Repeat every third third word you say say.

6. Give your claim to fame as having been nicknamed 'Festy' during high school.

7. Read a newspaper or book during the meal. Ignore your date.

8. Stare at your date's neck, and grind your teeth audibly.

9. Twitch spastically. If asked about it, pretend you don't know what they are talking about.

10. Stand up every five minutes, circle your table with your arms outstretched, and make aeroplane sounds.

11. Order a bucket of lard.

12. Ask for crayons to colour in the placemat. This works very well in fancier venues that use linen tablecloths.

13. Howl and whistle at women's legs, especially if you are female.

14. Recite your dating history. Improvise. Include pets.

15. Pull out a harmonica and play blues songs when your date begins to talk about themselves.

16. Eat soup with your hands.

17. When ordering, enquire as to whether the restaurant has any live food.

18. Without asking, eat off your date's plate. Eat more from their plate than they do.

19. Drool.

20. Chew with your mouth open, talk with your mouth full and spray crumbs.

21. Eat everything on your plate within thirty seconds of it being placed in front of you.

22. Excuse yourself to use the bathroom. Go back to the head waiter/hostess and ask for another table in a different part of the restaurant. Order another meal. When your date finally finds you, ask him/her 'What took you so long in the bathroom?!'

23. Recite graphic limericks to the people at the table next to you.

24. Ask the people at the neighbouring table for food from their plates.

25. Beg your date to tattoo your name on their derrière. Keep bringing the subject up.

26. Ask your date how much money they have with them.

215

27. Order for your date. Order something nasty.

28. Communicate in mime for the entire evening.

29. Upon entering the restaurant, ask for a seat away from the windows, where you will have a good view of all exits, and where you can keep your back to the wall. Act nervous.

30. Lick your plate. Offer to lick theirs.

31. Hum. Loudly. In monotone.

32. Fill your pockets with sugar packets, as well as salt and pepper shakers, silverware, floral arrangements…anything on the table that isn't bolted down.

33. Hold a debate. Take both sides.

34. Undress your date verbally. Use a megaphone.

35. Auction your date off for silverware.

36. Slide under the table. Take your plate with you.

37. Order a baked potato as a side dish. When the waiter brings your food, hide the potato, wait a few minutes, and then ask the waiter for that potato you 'never got'. When the waiter returns with another potato for you, have the first one back up on the plate. Repeat later in the meal.

38. Order beef tongue. Make lewd comparisons or comments.

39. Get your date drunk. Talk about their philosophy. Get it on tape, and use good judgement in editing to twist their words around.

40. Discuss boils and lesions, as if from personal experience.

41. Speak in pig Latin throughout the meal (or ubber-dubber language, or just nonsense).

42. Take a break, and go into the bathroom. When you return to the table, throw a spare pair of underwear on the back of one of the chairs. Insist that they just need airing out.

43. If they are paying, order the most expensive thing on the menu. Take one bite.

44. Bring twenty or so candles with you and during the meal get up and arrange them around the table in a circle. Chant.

45. Save the bones from your meal, and explain that you're taking them home to your invalid, senile old mother, because it's a lot cheaper than actually feeding her.

46. Order your food by colours and textures. Sculpt.

47. Take a thermos along, and hide it under the table. Order coffee, and fill the thermos one cup at a time.

48. Insist that the waiter cut your food into little pieces. In a similar vein, insist that he take a bite of everything on the plate, to make sure no-one has poisoned it.

49. Accuse your date of espionage.

50. Make odd allusions to dangerous religious cults.

51. Don't use any verbs during the entire meal.

52. Pass the hat in the restaurant. Use the proceeds (if any) to pay the bill.

53. Break wind loudly. Add colourful commentary. Bow.

54. Feed imaginary friends, or toy dolls you've brought along.

55. Bring a bucket along. Explain that you frequently get ill.

How to Avoid Disaster

So what do you think? Enough silly stories to make you feel better about your own love life? I have a few tips on how to avoid disaster if you're still worried.

Getting Your Mojo Happening

We all want someone we can relax and laugh with, and yet feel excited about. And that means we want people to feel that way about us.

Mojo begets mojo. The more dates you go on, the more mojo you will have. Start the ball rolling by getting a nice photo of yourself up on a few dating web sites. If there are three people calling or emailing you every day, desirability will begin to ooze from your every pore.

Spunks attract spunks. Even supermodels have to make some kind of an effort. If you want an extra boost of confidence, make yourself over. Ask a friend of the opposite sex to tell you when they thought you looked hot. Get a funky outfit, get a funky haircut and get to the gym. I can't say enough about the gym—it's packed with hotties, so it's a great perve, *and* you're making yourself gorgeous. Plus you walk out of there on a high. This also goes for all those sporty classes, and jogging. And fellas—get along to a yoga class for God's sake. They are packed with flexible women.

Approaching the Object of Your Desire

So you're out there, you've got some spunk happening and your mojo is through the roof. Now you can start to approach dates all by yourself in the real world.

Be yourself. You've heard it a million times. You need to have your own routine; your best friend's moves always look so try-hard. Sincerity and kindness are hot, shyness and awkwardness can also be charming. So long as you are thinking of the other person and how *they* feel (remember, it's not all about you) you can't go wrong really.

Here are some lines that really work:

Compliments are perfect when you say exactly what's on your mind, and you mean it. 'You are gorgeous', 'You're a babe', 'You are hot', 'You are beautiful', 'You look great'.

The best *staple line* that never fails to start a conversation and gives you all the info you need is: 'Hi, how are you going?' ('Yeah good'). 'Who are you here with?' (I'm here by myself/with my brother/it's my friend's birthday party').

Body language can be cool. A very slight 'I'm checking you out and I like what I see' nod with a cheeky smile works a treat even if you have been going out with the person for years. This move is hit and miss if you don't know each other but everyone likes to be on the receiving end.

The double take. This is a *solid gold manoeuvre*. Look at the person until they make eye contact, then look down shyly. Look again until they make eye contact, then smile. If they smile back, get on over there!

The Ask Out

The conversation ball is rolling, you still like them, and you want their number. The trick here is to ask them out as though you were asking to meet up with a new mate.

1. 'Hey, we should catch up sometime, what's your number?'
2. 'Do you want to go for a coffee (or lunch) this week? What's your number?'
3. 'Why don't you give me your number and I'll let you know when that concert/party/art exhibition is on.'
4. If you feel you must do a line on them, keep it simple. For guys (this makes girls melt), 'Would you like to have dinner with me sometime?' For girls (this makes guys laugh), 'So, shall we go on a date?'

The Phone Call

Yes wait, but not three days, not four days, and not a week. Wait two days only, and always call when you say you will.

If someone you like calls and you're busy, let them know they haven't been rejected: 'Well I'm busy tonight but…'

Dating Tips

Dating is playtime, so dates should be cruisey and allow room for spontaneity. Remember, they are more scared of you than you are of them so if someone you like calls and fumbles, give them a chance!

1. Treat your date like a friend and cut them some slack.
2. Don't make anyone give you a foot massage.
3. Don't ask for any kind of massage. It might be offered one day.
4. Don't spend your whole pay packet on a date, it puts too much pressure on the situation.
5. Don't take someone out with your friends on a wild night.
6. Be spontaneous but don't be wimpy and if they suggest something you are uncomfortable with, for God's sake say no and suggest something else.
7. If you are with mates and it's the first date, introduce them as a friend. Don't make gestures behind their back.
8. Don't play it cool by making the world a little colder. I have dated guys who hold out on compliments and warmth so they won't find themselves, 'wrapped around my finger' and they get *nowhere*.
9. Don't lie about your age.
10. If your mobile phone rings say 'Do you mind if I take this?' then turn it off.
11. Don't sit there texting, at all.
12. Give them your full attention and be courteous.
13. If you can't show up, call, even if it was just a drop in date.
14. Once you have established whether or not you are available for a relationship, don't make any analysis or announcements about the situation. Just keep that information to yourself, or if you really feel you have to, share it with your best friend.
15. Don't talk about exes; if it's too early, do not date.
16. Don't talk about your dog or cat or children too much.
17. Don't rush into anything. Wait and let the passion build.

18. Don't invite anyone new on a 'lesson' date (such as a salsa class).

19. Don't point out your negatives.

20. Don't even bring up negatives.

21. Listen.

22. Just be yourself, be nice and give it a go.

So there you go, you're ready to get out there and start playing the game. It's the best way to discover who you really are.

Suggested Reading

Web sites

www.rsvp.com.au Australia's biggest and best dating website.

www.gaydar.com.au Australia's biggest and best gay dating website.

Yahoo Dating: http://au.personals.yahoo.com/ Another very cool dating site.

www.dating.about.com This American website is fantastic for dating advice. The hostess, Brenda Ross, is brilliant (she is also the relationship adviser at **www.date.com**). Scroll down and check out the 'Dates From Hell Stories' link…you can post your own stories here.

http://www.drdating.com/ More dating advice. You can learn flirting tips or link to Lavalife.com.au for internet dating.

Books

Hot Love: how to get it by Tracey Cox. Tracey offers excellent tips on how to meet people and make your dates work.

The Kama Sutra by Vatsyayana. An oldie but a goodie. Well, why not? We can all improve…

The Rules by Ellen Fein and Sherrie Schneider.
http://www.therulesbook.com/ Take this book with a massive
grain of salt—it's prudish and ancient history, but it does teach a
lesson or two in self-respect.

The Art Of Seduction by Robert Greene. For those who need
help with seducing women.

Body Language Secrets: A Guide During Courtship & Dating
by R Don Steele. This is a book that gives you all the clues to
what's really going on in your date's head. It's available on
Amazon.com